Come ~ Celebrate Jesus!

Reflections for Advent and Christmastide
including
Special Feast Days, O Antiphons and Las Posadas

Francis X. Gaeta

Foreword by Msgr. Thomas Hartman

Resurrection Press
Mineola • New York

In Loving Gratitude to:
Fr. George B. Murphy, SJ
Sr. Joseph Agnes, SCH
Sr. Thelma Hall, RC
who showed me the face of Jesus.

First published in October 1997 by Resurrection Press, Ltd.
P.O. Box 248
Williston Park, NY 11596

Copyright © 1997 by Francis X. Gaeta

ISBN 1-878718-38-X
Library of Congress Cataloging-in-Publication Number 97-68863

Cover design by John Murello

Printed in the United States of America.

Contents

Foreword

FRANK GAETA IS A PRIEST'S PRIEST, a man's man, a shepherd of his flock, a pastor in the mold of Pope John XXIII. He leads by example. He believes in a God of love and mercy. He's available. He's kind. He cares.

It's no wonder that *Come, Celebrate Jesus!* is a gem. It's written for the believer who needs to be reminded of truths already known. It speaks to the mother and father who want their children to cherish the God of love. It gently invites those who are questioning, hurting, lonely, or needy to trust in God and not give up. It asks all of us to fear less, pray more and represent God well.

Fr. Frank lives in a busy, suburban parish. He loves sharing meals, buying gifts, and celebrating the lights, carols and the decorations of the Christmas season. He knows what it's like to be stressed out at Christmas time. He invites us, who are similarly stretched, to sit down with him during his morning meditation after Mass and benefit from the wisdom and experience of his "heart to heart" conversations with God.

He's so in love with the season that he wants to share some sage advice: Put aside ten percent of your gift-giving money for the poor. It will bring you closer to God. Make a good Confession. You'll feel better. Put aside fifteen minutes a day for Jesus. He will bring you peace and be a good friend. Make a list of four people with whom you've had a strained relationship. Give them a call. You'll be cooperating with God's desire to heal the brokenhearted. And, you might rekindle an old friendship.

For Fr. Frank, Advent is a time for quiet listening. It's a time to get ready for the birth of Jesus. Like the Magi we're invited to bring gifts to the Christ child. Like them we are asked to be willing to be inconvenienced. While they had to journey not always knowing where they were going, we might be asked to pray quietly a little bit each day not knowing exactly what will happen. As they brought gifts to share with the Holy Family, we might bring gifts to our family and the poor. As they gave glory to God, so we might do something special for God.

Fr. Frank spends a great deal of time in prayer in his own life. It gives him peace and energy and perspective. In meditation he learns to trust in God, to seek the will of God, and to see that his time and talents are meant to be used for God. It's out of this spiritual awareness that he speaks to us of God's unconditional love. As he looks at the cross he sees a Jesus who has suffered and who will be there for us when we suffer. He believes that God is there for the asking anytime we need help. He believes in God, trusts God and lives in God.

I particularly enjoyed his statement that it won't be until we die and meet God that we will know how precious, how good, and how beautiful we are and how deeply we are loved by God. These words ring so true. How comforting it would be if we were taught them with sincerity from our birth. There would be less pain, less fear, and more smiling faces in the world.

Spirituality for Fr. Frank is found in friendship with God and people. It's a cup of coffee, a meal, a prayerful liturgy spent together! He loves to be with people. He believes in community. For him God speaks through everyone. No one is to be dismissed. He says prophetically, "Every saint has a past and every sinner has a future." There's room in God's love for all of us.

Fr. Frank says that a saint is a sinner who never gives up. A saint is one who leads others to hope and to trust. These

6

are fine ideals for those of us who believe that we're here to "know, love, and serve God" while making a difference in this world.

—*Thomas Hartman*

Introduction

There is a Savior...
and He will light your way!

Dearest Friends,

I am so happy to offer you these meditations as springboards for prayer during the time of Advent and Christmas. I invite you to spend fifteen minutes every day in your Advent prayer. Try to do it at the same time and in the same place. This fifteen minutes of calm and tranquility has the power to transform all the frenetic hustle and bustle of our Christmas preparation into prayer and union with the Lord.

For each day of Advent I will cite the readings from the daily Mass. If you do not feel inclined to reflect on all the readings of the day, I urge you to be sure to read the Gospel (which is highlighted) very slowly. Ask yourself: "What is the Lord saying to me?" Then read the little commentary which is printed for each day. What does it say to you? What does it mean? Take a few minutes to turn it all over in your heart. You may conclude by praying the Lord's Prayer or the Hail Mary very slowly. That's all there is to it. Take the time. Fifteen minutes with Jesus each day will make this Advent a joy and a special gift to us all.

You will also find meditations for special feast days and the *O Antiphons*. These reflections will add to your Advent prayer and help in your preparation for Christmas.

Have a Blessed Advent and a very Merry Christmas!

In Jesus' Love,

Thank

Entering Advent in the Spirit of Henri Nouwen

WHAT YOU ARE READING, dear friends, at the beginning of this Advent/Christmas meditation book was the last thing that I wrote for it. I felt compelled to write it after reading Henri Nouwen's, *Can You Drink the Cup?* which was his last book. Although this Dutch born author died on September 21, 1996 (not in Advent), no one was more a person of the Incarnation and witness of the presence of Christ in everyone and everything. His spirit leads us peacefully and gently into this holy season.

Why is Henri Nouwen so special? Henri was the person who translated the Council and the new ecclesial and biblical spirituality into the language, images and experience of ordinary people. I glanced at the "Nouwen section" in my book case and found copies of twenty-two of his books! Henri was my teacher, mentor and spiritual director along with countless numbers of Christians who try to follow Jesus, serve His people and come to terms with the Church. He is especially a hero for me since he was a secular priest and ended his days as pastor to the l'Arche Daybreak Community in Toronto, a family of severely retarded adults and their friends and counselors. We priests are very proud of him and indebted to him. We all loved to poke fun at how expensive and skinny his books were!

Henri was totally honest but so gentle and sensitive to everyone. It is hard to imagine him ever deliberately hurting

11

another human being. He wrote so openly about his journey to God, about his struggles, sins, failures and victories. Even in the midst of tremendous success and fame he dealt with his own self-doubts, inadequacies and depressions. The spiritual life was not handed to him on a silver platter. Yet, in his writings and sharing he guided so many of us through the storms and uncertainties of the sixties and seventies. He taught us a new language of spirituality and faith. He helped us to preserve the best of the old and to embrace the new.

His theology was totally rooted in the Incarnation — the taking of flesh by Jesus. He taught us that this Incarnation is still happening and he touched the yearning in all of us for a Savior and for love and meaning in our lives. He made the most complicated things seem simple and understandable. He spoke to us in a language we could understand and that language flowed from a heart that had obviously been broken but was in the process of being healed. He finally realized that it could only be healed by Jesus in community. His last years at l'Arche gave him the family that brought him to life and prepared him to die.

Henri opened up exciting new possibilities by articulating what we were all experiencing but didn't know how to express. I will never forget the profound effect one of his concepts had on me. Reading his work *Creative Ministry* he warned about the minister expecting those he/she served to pay them for their ministry. When I began to read this section in the book I was put off. "The good minister doesn't work for pay," I thought. But sometimes we *do* expect recompense, not in money, but in the change of a person's life.

Henri powerfully taught us that all we could ever expect was the privilege to love and serve our people. We don't love them because they kick a habit of addiction or sin. We love them because they are worthy of our love. They are children of God. He taught us that we must try to love the way Jesus loved. I will never forget that lesson. I feel better now knowing that he is praying for me to accomplish it, because it's the toughest thing we are called to do — to love unconditionally, just as Jesus did.

While he led us into the desert of our hearts in prayer, he also taught us that real prayer and true holiness was in living life to the fullest. It was only in relationship that we could find the God for whom we longed. Henri found God in a profound manner as he lived among and served the humblest and most human needs of his family at l'Arche.

The great man of letters and books ultimately taught us that to love another person was, as Jean Valjean would remind us, "to see the face of God." We will find our God in the person next to us, not in any book or theory.

This intellectual giant finally found the God of love not in any library or church, but in tending to the physical and emotional needs of his l'Arche family. "Whatsoever you do to the least of my brothers, that you do unto me" (Mt. 25:40).

Can You Drink the Cup? concludes with this paragraph:

"The golden chalice (*of his ordination*) became a glass cup. But what it holds has remained the same. It is the life of Christ and our life, blended together into one life. As we drink the cup, we drink the cup that Jesus drank, but we also drink *our* cup. This is the great mystery of the Eucharist. The cup of Jesus, filled with his life, poured out for us and all people, and our cup, filled with our blood, have become one cup. Together when we drink that cup as Jesus drank it we are transformed into the one body of the living Christ, always dying and always rising for the salvation of the world."

Keep Christ In Christmas

AT THIS TIME OF YEAR we are subject to stern sermons warning us of the worldliness of the season and how far removed from the true spirit of Advent and Christmas most of what we do is. I'm not so sure. I'd like to offer some thoughts on how to observe and celebrate Advent and Christmas. It seems to me the key concept is balance. "In medio stat virtus."

Gift Giving

How far from the true spirit of Christmas can gift giving be? Is there a better way to celebrate the birthday of the King of Kings than by bringing a gift for someone we love? "Yes, but..." The "but" is the reminder that gift giving should not put us in debt. When it seems to be getting out of hand why not pray about what and how much we should give to our children and friends and family.

If it is becoming a burden — emotionally and financially — then it's time to re-evaluate. Is what I am doing making this a happier and holier time for me and my family? If not, evaluate and plan for a more Christ-like and joyous celebration.

Make sure that when you wrap your gifts you pray for the person who will receive the gift. Make every part of the experience an opportunity to thank God for the gift of this person.

If last-minute shopping in crowded malls makes you nervous and out of sorts, then find another way of doing it.

Shop in July or use catalogues. You are in control of how you spend your energy, time and money. Blame no one else if this beautiful time turns into a time of torture and distress.

The acid test to whether we understand the true meaning of gift giving will be whether we give at least ten percent of what we spend to the poor. Can't possibly afford that much? Then you probably don't get the real meaning of Christmas.

Christmas Cards

Make each card a prayer for the person who will receive it. As you sign each card "love," think of what it means to have the incredible grace of loving another person. Really make the card a prayer and an act of love.

Christmas Baking

Blessed is that house filled with an aroma of cookies baking. That aroma is the incense of the domestic. Happy the children of the mother (or father) who bakes and works at making a house a home — the little church.

Christmas Gatherings

How wonderful to get together with friends. Of course, you must be careful about drinking (and eating) too much. Don't drive when you've been drinking. But, again remember: Jesus did not use grape juice at the Last Supper. Respect brother alcohol and use him — never abuse him. When we use all of God's creation properly we praise Him and give Him glory.

Reconciliation

Advent is a natural time to make a good confession. Examine your conscience about your relationships — to yourself, to Jesus and to your neighbor. Let Jesus help you through the sacrament to heal any parts of your heart that are wounded or not at peace. Jesus wishes peace for you. Ask Him for that precious gift the angels announced to the shepherds —peace of mind and heart.

Another important form of reconciliation is for us to reach out to someone who has hurt us or whom we have hurt. Call someone each week of Advent whom you are "on the outs with." What a merry and blessed Christmas it will be if we do that!

Daily Prayer

The purpose of this little book is to get us to set aside fifteen minutes for Jesus each day. Are you too busy to pray? Then you *are* too busy and you do not have control over your life. When we make the time to pray each day we discover we have more time and better quality time. We have the opportunity to talk to Jesus about the shopping, cards, parties and all the things that make up this time when we pray each day. Try it. It will change your life.

Christmas is the most glorious day of the year. Christ is born to us as our Savior and Brother. We *must* celebrate His birth. Gifts, cards, celebration, parties are all wonderful ways to celebrate His presence in our lives and to rekindle old friendships. Celebrate it with all your heart! Make merry! Rejoice! Kill the fatted calf! But remember, all these wonderful things are meant to make us more generous, loving, compassionate and forgiving. The true Spirit of Christmas is found in Galatians 5:22, where Paul names the fruits of the Spirit: Charity, joy, peace, patience, endurance, kindness, generosity, faith, mildness and chastity. When these fruits of the Spirit are present the Lord can only be saying, "Keep the party going!" Merry Christmas and as Tiny Tim says, "God bless us everyone!"

Proper Readings of Advent

FIRST WEEK OF ADVENT

ADVENT IS ANOTHER EXAMPLE of Christian optimism. On every First Sunday of Advent we begin a new liturgical year. In all that she does and says the Church is speaking about the fact that we *can* begin again. We are not slaves of the past. The very fact that all the liturgical books begin on page one speaks of hope. Of course, we didn't get it all yet, but here we have a chance to begin again. It's OK not to know everything. How wise the Church is to remind us that while the process of conversion is never complete in us there is always the opportunity to begin again. Our God never withdraws His call or His love. We pray: "Come, Lord Jesus! Come to this world yearning for healing and peace. Come to me, Lord Jesus!" Part of me says, "What's the use?" What difference can a new year make? There are so many broken promises, so many incomplete projects, so many dreams unfulfilled, so many ideals compromised. In the midst of my lack of faith in my ability to change, a Child beckons and tells me not to give up. "Come, Lord Jesus!"

Maybe another year — this New Year — can make a difference. Maybe this will be the year that I will believe in and love myself the way the Lord Jesus does. Maybe this will be the best Christmas ever because I'll come to believe that Jesus is born every moment of my life.

First Sunday of Advent
Matthew 24:37–44; Mark 13:33–37;
Luke 21:25–28, 34–36

Today, Luke's Gospel speaks again of the end of the world. November is the month of the holy souls and the Church talks a great deal about our personal death and the "end of it all" when Christ, the Lord, returns to judge the living and the dead. It is a healthy thing to think and pray about these things.

Advent is a yearly reminder to look at our lives and dreams and to see if they are a part of the Kingdom of God. What does it profit someone to gain the whole world and lose one's soul in the process? There seems to be an unhealthy fear of the end times, the Rapture and even the year 2000 for some Christians. We are not called to be afraid. We are called to live — to live and to love as if each day were our last day. How different our lives would be if we did live that way. We would never put off saying those words of love, forgiveness and affirmation that we often postpone. Here is a very practical way to live in this "Incarnation" mode: Make a list of four people you've neglected or have been on the "outs" with and call one each week of Advent. What a different Christmas this will be because we have celebrated the sacrament of friendship four times!

Monday of the First Week of Advent
Isaiah 2:1–5; Psalm 122:1–8;
Matthew 8:5–11

The words of the centurion in today's Gospel have been immortalized by our Church. We pray them at each Mass before we receive Holy Communion: "Lord, I am not worthy to receive you but only say the word and I shall be healed." Jesus is amazed at the faith of this man. But it seems that Jesus was always very successful in touching the hearts of

18

those who were "on the outs." In the mystery of grace the non-believer often believes much more deeply than the "practicing" ones and the fruits of the Holy Spirit seem much more evident in their lives. The centurion speaks for each one of us — single parent, divorced, happily married, unhappily married, homosexual — all of us — "I am not worthy" — please just say the word and I shall be healed. The most beautiful moment of the week occurs when all the unworthy gather around the table and come to be fed. This meal is not a reward for good or moral living! It is rather, the sharing of the life and love of Him who loves us unconditionally. Jesus speaks the word to each of us that the centurion prayed for. We *are* healed! We *are* forgiven!

Tuesday of the First Week of Advent
Isaiah 11:1–10; Psalm 72:1, 7–8, 12–13, 17;
Luke 10:21–24

In the Gospel today Jesus tells us to look at what we have and to listen to the voices around us. Advent is the time of pondering what the mystery of the Incarnation means *now*. It's relatively easy to believe that the Word of the Father took flesh and was born of the Virgin two thousand years ago. The nativity scene is always so consoling and touching —just as it should be. But Bethlehem is just the beginning. Christ continues to take flesh in the people and events around us.

Now is the time to see Christ in the faces around us — spouses, children, co-workers, friends. Each of them is the face of Christ. Advent is a beautiful time to see the face of love in the faces we see every day and take for granted. It is the time to see the face of Jesus in the poor — the materially, spiritually, and emotionally wounded. It's the time to realize that the Body of Christ is called to heal the Body of Christ. Jesus takes flesh in *me*. I am the Incarnation. If I don't allow Jesus to live in me, there will be many people who will not touch Jesus. Jean Valjean's words touch our hearts at this holy time: "To love another person is to see the face of God."

Wednesday of the First Week of Advent
Isaiah 25:6–10; Psalm 23:1–3, 3–4, 5, 6;
Matthew 15:29–37

Jesus always seems to draw the same crowd — the poor, the crippled, the blind, the lepers and the beggars. Things really haven't changed much. Jesus is able to touch people's hearts because He preaches and lives the Gospel of love and acceptance. Jesus touches the hearts of those who need Him the most. The great tragedy of our spiritual lives occurs when we don't think we need a Savior. Religion can become a selfish venture that makes us *feel* good. The Eucharist and our prayer lives deteriorate into a "grace gaining" project to get us closer to God and to heaven. Jesus seemed to have a lot of trouble with people who needed themselves and their certainties more than they needed Him. Jesus feeds the crowds as a prelude to the times when He will feed the multitudes at the table of the Eucharist. Look who's at His table! Look who's at Mass! It's the poor, the crippled, the blind, the lepers, the beggars. *It's you and me.* He comes to us as food for sinners. He welcomes *everyone* to the table — no one excluded. The loaves and fishes in His hands feed everyone with plenty left over. Now the loaves and fishes in His hands are you and me. Through us He will feed the multitudes with plenty left over.

Thursday of the First Week of Advent
Isaiah 26:1–6; Psalm 118:1, 8–9, 19–21, 25–27;
Matthew 7:21, 24–27

Those who do the Father's will get to heaven. We all believe that, but what *is* the will of the Father? It is different for each of us. For one it is to marry and raise a family; for another it may be to end a marriage because of abuse or alcoholism. The will of God may mean living with the poorest of the poor for Mother Teresa, or working a second job for a mother or father to make sure their children have what they need.

How do I know God's will? By asking Him — by prayer. Prayer is an ongoing relationship and conversation with the Lord. When a man or woman is living the New Life, their whole life is lived with the Lord. They are always "heart to heart" with Jesus. There's no area of their lives that doesn't come to Jesus. Decisions are made by more than logic and common sense. They are made in Jesus as we try to acquire His mind and heart. When He's *always* in our heart, whether it's at the kitchen sink, the washing machine, in the car, or in the office, then we're *always* praying and we are *always* doing what the Father wants. All our decisions are talked over with Jesus. He has input into our job, how many children we should have, where we should live, etc. There's nothing we don't talk about with Him. That's prayer! And that's how we know what His will is for us.

Friday of the First Week of Advent
Isaiah 29:17–24; Psalm 27:1, 4, 13–14;
Matthew 9:27–31

"Son of David, have pity on us." It has been said that we never really pray until we are at rock bottom — until we're desperate. The two blind men in the Gospel today prove the point. They know that this is their one and only chance to meet Jesus and to make their request. They ignore all of the negative people around them who assure them that Jesus has no time for them. Nothing will keep them quiet. "Have pity on us!" That's how we have to pray — with all our hearts — with everything we have. But voices try to quiet us, too. We hear voices that say: "O sure, you come to Him when you need Him; where were you when things were go-

21

ing great?" "How can you have the nerve to pray? You're not worthy to pray!" "Get your act together first then you can think about a relationship with him." But our Jesus says to us as He did to the blind man, "Do you believe I can do this?" We respond, "Yes, Lord, I do believe." Jesus touches our eyes so gently and tells us to look at His face. We see His love for us and we know we can never allow ourselves to be blind again.

Saturday of the First Week of Advent
Isaiah 30:19–21, 23–26; Psalm 147:1–6;
Matthew 9:35–10:1, 6–8

Jesus is on the go. He goes from town to town to meet His people and to tell them the Good News — God loves them unconditionally and always. It's beautiful to see that He doesn't usually wait for His people to come to Him. He takes the initiative. He reaches out. He says "hello" first. He smiles and welcomes. He has all the time in the world to sit down and have a cup of wine. The schedule doesn't matter. The person with Him right now is all that's important.

Jesus calls for laborers to gather the harvest with Him. The call for vocations is not a call for more managers and bureaucrats or bigger and better programs. Jesus is calling for shepherds who have a real relationship with their sisters and brothers and who truly love them. We really only respond to the invitation and the call when we know that we are loved and that we are important for who we are. There are enough efficient and capable professionals in the world already. Jesus is calling for lovers to take care of His flock — He wants lover-parents, lover-priests, lover-lay ministers. He wants a group of laborers who are so thrilled by knowing that God loves them that they can't help but to give that love away.

SECOND WEEK OF ADVENT

JOHN THE BAPTIST and Our Lady are the two figures who lead us through Advent to Jesus. They are very different but complement each other. John represents the active part of our personality and Mary the contemplative part.

John is the man of action. He is at the River Jordan baptizing and preaching. He is calling people to a new way of thinking and living. He calls people to make radical changes in their lives and in their ways of relating to others. He calls us beyond charity to justice. He reminds us that it is not enough to simply be charitable but we must seek what is just, what people deserve because they are human beings. We, too, are called to Christian activism. We are expected to be doers of the Word not just hearers. The Christian is expected to work hard, to lay down his/her life in service to the community. The Christian has to be busy in building the Kingdom — the City of God — the Kingdom of Peace, Justice and Love.

John reminds us not to rest on our laurels, not to become self-satisfied or lazy. He calls us to a simple life, a life built not on materialism but on the values of people. As we are tempted to overspend this Christmas, John in his rough coat of camel's hair with a leather belt around his waist enjoying the fine dining of locusts and grasshoppers reminds us that we have to work for a more simple life and share what we have with the poor. There is a big difference between what we need and what we want. In Advent, John reminds us that most of our sisters and brothers *never* get what they *need* for a decent life.

Second Sunday of Advent
Matthew 3:1–12; Mark 1:1–18;
Luke 3:1–6

John the Baptist is up to his old tricks again — making us feel guilty! He is the one who truly afflicts the comfortable. He demands that we look at the patterns of our behavior and the values from which they flow. What do we *really* believe in? Whom do we *really* prepare for? John tells us to prepare the way for the Lord. He tells us that valleys must be filled, hills leveled, winding paths made straight and rough ways smooth. It all boils down to hard work — the *process* of conversion and change of heart. What is lacking in our hearts must be filled in. Perhaps we are becoming too hard, too business-like or too cold. We need a dose of compassion and tenderness. We have to take more time with relationships. Most of us have no time because we work so hard. We do good things but too much of even good things tends to deaden our desire to grow in love with family and friends. John calls us not just to fill in what's lacking but to cut away what shouldn't be in our hearts. That really hurts! The prejudice, greed, lust, laziness — it all has to go if we would have a heart that's ready to receive the Child this Christmas. Conversion hurts. Change hurts. But if we are not willing to do some work on ourselves this Advent, the birth of our Savior will not be able to have the effect in our hearts and lives that it should. By the way, who will you call this week to renew or fix up a strained relationship?

Monday of the Second Week of Advent
Isaiah 35:1–10; Psalm 85:9–14;
Luke 5:17–26

This Gospel is a classic! They just will not leave Jesus alone — lowering the paralytic through the roof so that Jesus would heal him! It's Jesus' own fault. That's what He gets for loving people and showing them the power of that love. The dilemma of Jesus is the dilemma of any of His true disciples. Tremendous, and sometimes unreasonable demands are made upon us. The heart of our lives consists in ministering to others.

The life of a parent, spouse, priest and friend must always be defined in the loving and generous gift of our talents and time to others. It is true that we must care for ourselves, but the meaning and the joy of our lives will come from the gift of ourselves to others. We are called like Jesus *to* serve, not *to be* served. Once we start there is no stopping.

Notice what the Lord says to the paralytic in the Gospel. After He heals him He gives him a job — pick up your mat; go home; get on with your life; start healing others. That's how it is with us. He heals us; He loves us and then He gives us a job — to do the same for others, to give the gifts away. The next time someone removes the tiles from your roof to place someone at your feet for healing, just remember how they did it to Jesus and chuckle as you remember you're only getting what you asked for!

Tuesday of the Second Week of Advent
Isaiah 40:1–11; Psalm 96:1–3, 10–13;
Matthew 18:12–14

Jesus begins this story of the Good Shepherd seeking after the one lost sheep by asking: "What is your thought on this?" It's safe to say that when you happen to be the lost sheep, it's wonderful to know that Jesus loves you so much. Unfortunately, we don't come across enough as the Church of compassion seeking out the lost sheep and welcoming them home. Yet the truth is we are never more part of the Church and never more loved by the Lord than when we seek out the lost. Jesus tells us repeatedly that He comes for the sick and the sinner. His ministry is to invite home those who are in despair and alienated from God and the Church.

This loving compassion of Jesus reaches out to us as the spark of conversion begins to burn, but it also reaches out to us when we're not yet able to change as we might want to. His Church is filled with the virtuous, but also with the struggling and the broken desperately yearning for a Savior —who loves them not for what they do or don't do, but for who they are.

We have all been that sheep that Jesus saved. Because of that we make our lives and our ministry the continuation of the life of Jesus the Good Shepherd. But it's easy to forget what it's like to be all alone in the briars or in the gutter. It's so easy to forget what life was like before He picked us up and carried us home. What a tragedy that is! When we forget our past we make the Church a respectable place of the clean and the righteous rather than the refuge of the dirty, the poor and the broken-hearted —all those who yearn for a savior. Remember *every* saint has a past and *every* sinner has a future.

Wednesday of the Second Week of Advent
Isaiah 40:25–31; Psalm 103:1–4, 8, 10;
Matthew 11:28–30

"Come to Me." This Gospel is one to be pondered over and over. It is an invitation from One who loves us without condition. It is an invitation from the Lord reminding us that He is always there for us and that His love is greater than any force or enemy in our lives. As we pray about these words of Jesus let's think of them in terms of Jesus calling us to forgiveness. A very special part of every Advent is sacramental confession. At the heart of that sacrament is the mystery of our God's forgiveness.

How confused we are when we pray for forgiveness. We pray as if the Lord is angry and we will change His mind and thus we will be forgiven. God's attitude to us never changes. He always loves us. There is not a moment when

26

He is not pouring His love into our hearts. Forgiveness really means a changed me. I pray for the grace to accept what God is constantly giving to me — His love and forgiveness. Conversion consists in acquiring a heart that accepts the gift of love that the Lord is constantly offering to me.

When Jesus says, *"Come,"* He is saying . . . *Believe Me. Trust Me. I am on your side. I will never, I can never withdraw the gifts of love or forgiveness that I promised you on the cross.* In that love is the rest we seek and the peace that can be found nowhere else. Come to Him this Advent. Let His love fill your heart. Don't be afraid anymore. The Son of God comes to us as an infant. How can we ever be afraid of a little baby?

Thursday of the Second Week of Advent
Isaiah 41:13–20; Psalm 145:1, 9, 10–11, 12–13;
Matthew 11:11–15

Matthew's Gospel today gives us only a hint of how precious and blessed we are as part of the Kingdom. Jesus tells us that John the Baptist is the greatest man history has ever known, but the *least* born into His Kingdom is greater. It is so important that *before* we look at our sins and failures we look at who we are. Each of us is another Christ. We are born into His Body at holy baptism. The Father looks at us and sees Jesus. We are flesh of His flesh and bone of His bone. We are the Body of Christ.

It is in knowing our identity (who I am) that I can know what I must do (my destiny). If I claim my identity and make it the foundation and motivating power of my life then my actions follow naturally and I am compelled to *be* Christ in my everyday life.

Our quest in life is to discover more completely the Christ who dwells within us and to allow Him to live in us more fully. The spiritual life will always direct us to constantly discover and believe more completely in who I am (Christ), and then live accordingly. Everything I ever do in life will flow from my constant discovery of my identity.

T.S. Eliot said it so beautifully:

> "We shall not cease from exploration.
> And the end of all our exploring
> Will be to arrive where we started.
> And know the place for the first time."
> —*Four Quartets* (*Little Gidding*)

Friday of the Second Week of Advent
Isaiah 48:17–19; Psalm 1:1–6;
Matthew 11:16–19

Jesus echoes a very common complaint of leaders: "You're damned if you do, and you're damned if you don't." Obviously Jesus did not appreciate being called a glutton and a drunkard. This is what His enemies would call Him for the style of ministry that He had adopted. Jesus' favorite way to reach people seems to be table ministry. He accepted many invitations to eat and drink with people. Remember, in His day eating meant a lot more than fulfilling a biological need. It was much more than the activity of strangers eating lunch at the same diner counter. Eating and drinking was sacramental. It meant a communion and a bond of friendship with your fellow diners. As Jesus eats and drinks with the sinners, He is saying by the very action that He loves them and they are important. But Jesus eats with everybody — prostitutes, tax collectors, Pharisees — *everybody* is part of the Church. *Everybody* has a seat at the Lord's table. Sunday Mass continues this table ministry of Jesus. He continues to welcome everybody there who seeks Him. There is always a place there for us. So Jesus takes it on the chin for what He does. So will we. Remember, our life is not to be lived to please others, but to please the Lord. Jesus could take the flack and so can we!

28

Saturday of the Second Week of Advent
Sirach 48:1-4, 9–11; Psalm 80:2-3, 15–16;
Matthew 17:10–13

Today's Gospel opens up a theme that we don't think much about during Advent — that of suffering. Jesus refers to the sufferings of Elijah, John the Baptist and His own future sufferings. We are accustomed to thinking about suffering in terms of the homeless, the hungry and all those suffering from material hardship in the Christmas Season. But, for many, emotional pain can be even greater suffering. For many people the holidays are hell. This time of year which is centered on family and home, accentuates the pain and loneliness of those who have painful marriages, are divorced, or are dealing with depression, sickness, or the loss of a loved one. Instead of experiencing peace on earth, the holidays are salt in the wounds of what *could* have been. Yet, Jesus is savior to all.

The very fact that Jesus comes to us as a homeless person, leaves His country as a political refugee and identifies with the poor, reminds us that He comes to hold and comfort those whose hearts are broken. Jesus is savior first to those who have nothing. He is by the side of those who have lost the things that truly matter — love, family, and friends. We are reminded by the coming of Jesus that as we make our preparations for Christmas, we do so with great sensitivity to those whose hearts are broken. We try to make the season a little more bearable by being there for them. Our Church proclaims a savior who has suffered everything so that we will believe that He is really there for us when we hurt and have nothing.

THIRD WEEK OF ADVENT

THIS WEEK WE REFLECT upon the great Advent figure, the prophet Isaiah. As the Church proclaims his tender and gentle description of the Messianic Kingdom one is filled with a sense of what the Lord wants for this world — the Kingdom of Peace and Justice. Pope Paul VI told the world that if it *"wanted peace it must work for justice."* We have always been a Church of tremendous charity. One need only look at the number of institutions in the United States dedicated to charity: schools, orphanages, asylums, hospitals, homes, etc.

At this time of the Holy Spirit the Church is taking a very important step in asking *why* people are poor and what must be done to change the unjust structures that allow and perpetuate this institutional injustice. Mother Teresa would be the best example of the Church's giving charity while Archbishop Romero would well represent the Church seeking justice. Of course, they exist hand in hand. *It's not either/or — it's both/and.*

As we read the prophet Isaiah we are touched by his revolutionary vision. It is a new order in which the poor have rights and all people are called to work for the establishment of these rights. The Spirit of Isaiah also leads to a new and life-giving understanding of Eucharist. We come to understand that our celebration of Eucharist will be incomplete until we have brought peace and justice to all people. Advent is a reminder that we are called to create the new world order according to the vision of Isaiah. Things like voting, studying the political issues, reading, reverence for the environment, participation in community organizing — all become very real and powerful religious pursuits. Isaiah teaches us that our faith and religion are incomplete without them.

Please note: There are special readings beginning on the seventeenth of December through Christmas. These readings and meditations replace the proper readings and they begin on page 39.

Third Sunday of Advent
Matthew 11:2–11; John 1:6–8, 19–28;
Luke 3:10–18

Gaudete! Rejoice! We're halfway there. Jesus is truly coming to us. This third Sunday is a reminder to us that Jesus is the source of our joy and that we must have hope. So often Christians appear to be the prophets of gloom and despair in the world rather than the proclaimers of the Good News. We are all aware of the evil that surrounds us. Our daily newspapers are filled with war and violence. Yet, we believe that Christ has come and that we have the answer — love. This love is the meaning of our lives. It is the only thing that works. It is the only thing that Jesus asks of us.

As the liturgy calls us to rejoice today, it calls us to share the dream of Jesus and to put into practice in concrete ways the love of Jesus Christ. We are called to love one another and to lay down our lives for one another. The only people who ever really experience joy are those who give their lives — a little each day — for others. We know where we have to begin — in our own hearts, our own marriages, our own family, our own job. As we go out of ourselves and take the extra step, we allow Jesus to be born again and we unleash the power of His love and joy in this world.

As we get closer to Christmas we should be getting closer to the people we love. We bring them the joy of Jesus. Who will you reach out to this week? Let's begin with ourselves. Do we care for ourselves, physically and psychologically? The best gift some people ever give themselves is a decision to go for counseling to work through a problem that is oppressing them. That's real joy! That's how Jesus wants us to love ourselves. We can share that love this week by calling that special person that we have hurt or neglected.

Monday of the Third Week of Advent
Numbers 24:2–7, 15–17; Psalm 25:4–5, 6–7, 8–9;
Matthew 21:23–27

In today's Gospel Jesus is questioned about authority. It's a deep and penetrating question because it reveals so much of what we believe and who we are. We often mistake power for authority. Power is the ability to have what you want and to force other people to do what you want. Money, armies, fame and popularity can give a person power. Indeed, in our world money can get you almost anything you want — except authority. Authority is the power a person has because of who he/she is. When we talk about authority we talk about people like Mother Teresa, Dorothy Day, John XXIII, Oscar Romero and Pope John Paul. These blessed saints have little of what moves the wheels of the modern world, but they have a power to touch hearts and to lead people to a greatness they never dreamed they were capable of. The modern saint whose heart is filled with the love of God and neighbor possesses power that compels us to faith and trust. The real authority of this world rests in the most unlikely places — in the simple and poor who seek peace and justice, in the loving and faithful who live out their commitment no matter what, in the prophets who sow the seeds of unity and peace and reconciliation. Our call is to be men and women of great authority who follow the example of a Lord who is delighted to be servant and to wash the feet of the poor.

Tuesday of the Third Week of Advent
Zephaniah 3:1–2, 9–13 Psalm 34:2–3, 6–7, 17–19;
Matthew 21:28–32

Today's Gospel leaves out a third son/daughter type — the one who said "yes" and actually did go out to the vineyard and stayed through thick and thin and never gave up and never stopped loving, but learned to love even more. There *are* saints like that. You know them when you see them. The fire of their baptism has never been quenched. It burns brighter each day. We all have them in our lives. Their innocence doesn't make them cold or aloof — just the opposite. They are the most loving, most forgiving, most tolerant of all. Their extraordinary love and passion for the Lord inspires the son/daughter — number one and two types — to have hope in the all-consuming, powerful and brilliant fire of God's love. They are an inspiration and encouragement to the rest of us never to give up, never to stop trying and always to believe that there is a God of love and mercy who will *never* let go of us. The smile of these holy ones changes a dark day into one of hope. Their word of encouragement makes anything possible. They are the closest thing on this earth to Christ Himself. They are the Incarnation repeated time and time again. Jesus Christ continues to take flesh in them. They give us hope and their lives are the promise to us that we can do it, too.

Thirty-two years ago I met one of these saints, Sister Joseph Agnes, a woman of complete self-giving to her kids. She promised me that day that she would offer the fourth decade of her rosary each day for me. All through the years she has kept her promise. I know that's why I am still a priest and I am writing this tonight. Thank the Lord for the saints in your life. And remember, *you* are probably someone's special saint.

Wednesday of the Third Week of Advent
Isaiah 45:6–8, 18, 21–25; Psalm 85:9–14;
Luke 7:18–23

"Go tell John what you see," says Jesus to John's disciples. Jesus proceeds to elaborate on this by describing the signs of the Messianic Kingdom — the blind see, the lepers are cleansed, the crippled walk, the deaf hear, the dead are raised and the poor have the Gospel preached to them. All these things they see for themselves. Jesus must be the "One Who is to come."

This "Seeing is Believing" is a very good test of the Kingdom. What do we see when we look into our own hearts? Is the kingdom in me, or do I belong to someone else? What do we see when we look at our families, our parishes, our Church? Is it obvious to all that Jesus is Lord? Is this truly His Church? Are we His true faithful followers with burning hearts seeking justice and peace for all people? Many look at us and they don't know what to think. We can be more interested in power, money and comfort than in the simple life and service of Jesus Christ. We can be more interested in controlling people than serving them. (The fact that so many don't feel at home with us should make us very concerned.) The fact that some must look for Jesus elsewhere because they don't find Him in us should make us afraid of the day when He returns, arm in arm, with the homosexuals, the prostitutes, the divorced, the single parents, the AIDS sufferers and all the others we turned away, ignored, or refused to give the Eucharist. On that day He will ask us, "What have you done to my Church?" What will we answer Him? There's still time to make sure that the Kingdom is established *at least* in my own heart.

Thursday of the Third Week of Advent
Isaiah 54:1–10; Psalm 30:2–6, 11–13;
Luke 7:24–30

Jesus tells us today that the least born into the Kingdom of God is greater than John the Baptist. The words of Jesus are hard to fathom, hard to understand, but they are true. We are even greater than John. How? Through God's call and grace.

We are called to holiness — to live a new life — as we follow Jesus. So often we think that the Church will make us

34

holy, but we *already* are holy. Our baptism has consecrated us into the priesthood of Jesus Christ. As we hear His call and follow Him in our life and vocation we already possess holiness in our marriage, parenthood, love and relationships. Our Church's role is to remind us of what we *already* possess—God in our life. Our quest is to become more aware of what we are and what we already possess—the Kingdom of God within us.

This holy awareness grows as we begin to understand that our spouse is Jesus and as we realize that love in all its dimensions — spiritual, emotional, physical, sexual — is sacred and holy. As we hold and love our spouse and children, as we work for them, we do something so holy and so beautiful—we touch Jesus and we love Jesus. This is the life of the least born into the Kingdom. This is a sacramental life of grace as we become more aware of the holiness of that which we touch. This Advent we look at all creation and see there the presence of God and the threshold of holiness.

Friday of the Third Week of Advent
Isaiah 56:1–3, 6–8; Psalm 67:2–3, 5, 7–8;
John 5:33–36

The Christmas Season has always used lights — many of them as signs of the presence of the King. Today Jesus describes John as the lamp set ablaze and burning bright. Jesus referred to his followers as the Light of the World. When we walk with Jesus we love the light. We have nothing to fear. Our lives are transparent. It is this kind of freedom to which Jesus calls us. The Truth loves the light. The liar loves the shadows and darkness.

In this holy time, Jesus invites us to walk with Him in the brightness and freedom of truth. He calls upon His friends to live for others — to proclaim His truth — truth in all the areas and parts of our lives. He calls us to be truthful with ourselves, to be honest and up front when we pray and talk to our God. True prayer is like the prayers we find in the psalms — filled with exaltation, praise, joy and moments of doubt, anger and cursing. They are real prayers in which we tell our God the Truth. This light/truth attitude flows into our daily life as we say what we mean and mean what we say. The more powerful the institution, the more difficult it becomes to tell the truth. It took us five hundred years to admit the truth of the Galileo affair! Jesus calls his disciples to the simple and honest life in which the truth is always obvious and in which there is never a need to cover up, hide, conceal or tell a lie. The truth sets us free. As the light of Christ shines in our lives we brighten the way for so many who will not stumble because we are the truth, we are the light. Jesus never has anything to hide. Do you?

FOURTH WEEK OF ADVENT

THIS SUNDAY THE GENTLE and loving presence of Mary makes itself felt in the liturgy and the very heart of the Church preparing for Christmas. Last Sunday, John the Baptist, the activist, led us *outside* of ourselves making us aware of our personal responsibility to change ourselves and our world. Today, Mary, representing the contemplative side of our personalities, leads us *inward* to discover the Jesus who is there.

Much of our prayer and reflection about Mary during Advent centers on her pregnancy. Mary is the true contemplative as she listens to and feels the heartbeat of Jesus within her. Mary invites us to listen with her to Jesus. That listening requires quiet and space. It requires us to enter into our inner core to hear Him who is always within us and always wanting to share His peace with us. Christian contemplation is becoming aware of Him who is always present within us, but whom we seldom hear because we drown out the sound of His heartbeat by the frenetic pace of our lives. Advent is about quiet listening. It is an opportunity to allow the presence of Jesus to transform our lives, but it demands quiet. Maybe we're afraid of being quiet because of what Jesus might say to us or ask of us. The beautiful image of the Mother "hearing" and "feeling" God within her should dispel all fear. What could the child ever say to us but that He loves us? Don't be afraid of the One who loves you the most.

Fourth Sunday of Advent
Matthew 1:18–24; Luke 1:26–38;
Luke 1:39–45

Mary is really the first Christmas card. She brings the greetings of peace and love to Elizabeth. As our preparations for Christmas become intense, it's a good time to reflect on what we are about and why.

Let there be no doubt about it: what we do to prepare for and celebrate the birth of our Savior is good! The baking and cooking, the cards and gift wrapping, the parties and the shopping are all good things. But we do have to ask ourselves whether we go to excess in celebrating.

Maybe we should look to a few guidelines to our celebrating (see pp. 14–16). Will we go heavily into debt? Will we go through the motions and not really have love and personal presence in the cards we send and the gifts we give? Are we taking a few moments each day in prayer? Are we reaching out to the person we're "on the outs" with? Will we tell people we love how we feel about them? *Will we remember the poor in a real, sacrificial and personal manner?* The answer to these questions should agree with those of Jesus.

In the touching Gospel of the Visitation, Mary goes to "help out" her older, pregnant cousin Elizabeth. Mary teaches us how important and how holy the seemingly ordinary is. Take time in these busy days to bring the Jesus within you to some friend or relative who is homebound or who just needs to see your smiling face and who would love to have a nice cup of coffee with you.

Special Readings — December 17 to 24

December 17
Genesis 49:2, 8–10; Psalm 72:3–4, 7–8, 17;
Matthew 1:1–17

The genealogy of Jesus is a delight to read. St. Matthew writes for his Jewish audience making a point for his audience by fooling around with the number seven (David). He shows that Jesus born of Mary is a true descendant of David in the Messianic line. He also places in the genealogy of Jesus some very disreputable persons as he makes the point that Jesus has come *from* sinners *for* sinners. The real and true humanity of Jesus is a very important factor for Matthew and his audience, and for us.

This Jesus is one of us. He enters our world to bear our burdens, to live our life, to be one with us in all things but sin! Jesus shares the emotional, physical and psychological makeup that we do. He *really* laughs and cries. He *really* knows fear, loneliness and the hurt of betrayal. Jesus is not a good actor going through the motions of being human. He *is* human. He shares all the joys and the burdens of being human to show us that he understands what we're going through and to tell us how beautiful it is to be human. Even the painful moments of our lives are moments of unspeakable beauty because they are so human. Often as I celebrate a funeral Mass, I pray with a family whose hearts are broken and I tell them how blest they are to love their

39

mother, father or spouse so much. The most sacred moments of life are those in which we deeply experience love, life and death. When we do we are most like our Jesus — fully alive and fully human. The more we deny our feelings, joys and hurts, the more we bury them and fail to deal with them, the less human we are and the less like Jesus.

December 18
Jeremiah 23:5–8; Psalm 72:1, 12–13, 18–19;
Matthew 1:18–24

The Gospel today portrays in just a few words the crisis and test that so many face in the modern world: "Before they lived together she was found to be with child" (Mt. 1:18). What would have become of all of us if Mary had decided that the life within her was just "a mass of tissue" and disposed of it with an abortion? Nonetheless it is so unfortunate that so much of the Church pro-life rhetoric today never really speaks of the main issue — the fetus is a human being filled with hope, promise and an unlimited future — just like the fetus inside Mary's body.

We fail so miserably to preach a real pro-life Gospel because we only seem to be concerned about abortion. What about our ministry to those women and men who are terrified because of an unplanned pregnancy? "Who will take care of my children?" "How can I keep my job?" "I just can't afford another child." "He'll throw me out if I'm pregnant again." These are the real cries of anguish of many of our sisters and brothers who choose an abortion.

While the world becomes poorer as each potential Christ Child is aborted, we as a Church seem to be insensitive to *all* the issues that are part of a pro-life stance. Poverty, housing, jobs, nutrition, drugs, crime — *all* of these issues are part of the larger abortion issue. Perhaps the greatest issue of all is that we are not preaching a fully, totally consistent life doctrine — the seamless garment — to our young. In the long run that will cost us even more than abortion itself.

December 19
Judges 13:2–7, 24–25; Psalm 71:3–6, 16–17;
Luke 1:5–25

Reading this Gospel of Elizabeth's pregnancy makes one think about the tough times that children and family life are up against today. What was considered the greatest blessing possible to a couple — a child — is today often thought of as a curse. Couples who are pregnant have to give an explanation for bringing children into the world. Many times, they have the cost and the inconvenience that a child will bring thrown into their faces.

Advent is a reminder that the greatest blessing and calling that God can give us is to bring children into this world. As we look at the Christ Child we are all filled with deep emotion. This baby touches every good thing within us. But, every child is the Christ Child! Every child is the promise that God's mercy and love to us are without end. How precious loving parents are to God. The most beautiful gift parents can ever give their children is that they love each other. Christmas is such a powerful statement that marriage and parenting are the most precious and religious activities we can ever be a part of. The man and woman giving their whole life and love to this vocation are the saints in our world today. The Church does not *make* them holy — it reminds them of the holiness that they already possess and encourages them to keep going.

I think at the top of the Litany of Saints are those holy people who choose to keep their child rather than abort it and the single parents who raise their children with so much love. Jesus is truly among us in their holy lives.

December 20
Isaiah 7:10–14; Psalm 24:1–6;
Luke 1:26–38

Today we have the pleasure of reading the same Gospel we read on December 8 —the magnificent Gospel of the Annunciation. On December 8, we reflected on the "yes" of Mary and how it changed all of human history and how our "yes" can do the same. Today, let's just think about Mary. Why do *you* love her so much? Why is she so special and important to *you?*

When I begin to explain what Mary means to me, theology and scripture become inadequate. In fact, they get in the way. I believe that the only way one can appreciate Mary is by either being, or having, or wishing for a loving mother. For me personally, much of this flows from my own mother and sisters and my relationship with them.

The most beautiful home without a mother is just a house. There is a warmth, healing, health, joy and encouragement only a mother can bring. When mom is home everything is OK. We all wait for her to come home and then we relax. When she comes home everything is back to normal. The heart and the warmth is restored. Peace flows to everyone in that house because the house has again become home.

The future of our world will depend upon mothers being mothers *first* before career or anything else. The love of a mother is so powerful, so sacramental, so transforming, that to grow up without it can leave wounds that may never be healed. That's what Mary means to the Church. Could we do the Lord's work without her? Of course! But if we did we would be a cold, efficient salvation machine doing a job but depriving people of the feminine, motherly passionate love of God. Mary has kept the Church human —without her the most beautiful church is a house but not a home.

December 21

Song of Solomon 2:8–14 or Zephaniah 3:14–18;
Psalm 33:2–3, 11–12, 20–21; **Luke 1:39–45**

Today we have the joy of hearing the Visitation Story. We again witness the visit of the *Virgin* who is with child to the *married woman* who is with child. We know that when the Church proclaims Mary as "Ever Virgin," she is speaking of more than physical virginity. The virginity of Mary is much more a spiritual virginity, meaning that Mary is committed and belongs to God more than to any earthly relationship or bond. Mary's virginity is a model of our own virginity whether we are married or single. Each Christian must have a part of her/himself that belongs totally and exclusively to God.

At the same time, each Christian must be "married" in the sense that we all must live out our love of God by loving real flesh and blood people. We must be committed to *someone.* A virgin who doesn't love anybody in particular but everybody in general just isn't loving. I must love *my* husband, *my* wife, *my* children, *my* parishioners, *my* students, *my* friends, etc. or I am loving no one and my virginity is just an excuse for a frigid and selfish life-style.

Mary, our model, is the Virgin Wife-Mother. The depth of her love of Joseph, Jesus and the Church flows from the sacred place in her heart in which only God is found. Her life reminds us, especially at this holy time, that we must be "virgin" and "married" at one and the same time. Speak to her today about how you will accomplish this.

December 22

1 Samuel 1:24–28; 1 Sam 2:1, 4–8;
Luke 1:46–56

Today we are thrilled to read Mary's glorious Magnificat in Luke's Gospel. The Scripture reading of the Visitation begun yesterday is completed today. Every believer must know that this great hymn of Mary is our hymn. Mary, our sister, speaks on behalf of all the "little ones," the "anawim" — the poor, the downtrodden, the widow, the orphan, the foreigner, the exiled, the homeless, the street person, the person with AIDS, etc.! She speaks the prophetic word for all who place God and His holy will at the heart of their being. As Mary praises God for what He will do for the poor, that poverty is more than the lack of material things; it harkens back to our concept of her virginity — being totally open to or belonging to God. As Mary exalts and praises the poor whom God lifts up, she identifies with all those who suffer on this earth this Christmas. We specifically mentioned people who are on the fringe of society. Our world ignores and despises most of them. They are the non-persons. But in each of our lives there have been times when we were all like these sisters and brothers. There were times when the pain was so unbearable we thought that we would die and we literally did not know how we could go on another day. *We* were homeless, the street person, the addict, etc., etc.

Mary, our Mother, spoke for us and sang the song of our salvation as she said, "He raised up the lowly to high places." The Lord continues to raise up those who are truly poor and who belong to Him.

December 23
Malachi 3:1–4, 23–24; Psalm 25:4–5, 8–10, 14;
Luke 1:57–66

"His name is John." What's in a name? Everything. Names seem to fit their owners very well. It's hard to imagine the people we know with any other name. They just seem to fit. Most of us can trace a series of names that have been given to us as we've grown up. I went from Fran to Frannie to Francis to Frank — but to the people who really know me from "way back when," it's always Fran or Frannie. As names evolve, people are telling us what they see in us and what they think about us.

What your parents call you is your true and real name — so I think down deep I'll always be Fran or Frannie. Our God calls us by our true name. Only He knows what it is! God calls us by name because we are so unique and special to Him. There's no other like us — never was and never will be. So deep is that precious love that He has carved it on the palm of His hand (Isaiah 43).

What is more beautiful than to hear our name spoken by someone who loves us? When they speak our name with love it really is a prayer. When God speaks our name at the end of our life it will be the moment when we will completely know how precious, good and beautiful we are and how deeply loved we are by our God.

> *"What will this child be?*
> *Was not the hand of the Lord upon Him?"*
> —Luke 1:66

Christmas Eve — December 24
2 Samuel 7:1–5, 8–11, 16; Psalm 89:2–5, 27, 29;
Luke 1:67–79

Yesterday's Gospel of Luke about the naming of John is brought to a conclusion in the beautiful and touching Canticle of Zechariah. Zechariah praises the Lord for the birth of his son John and proceeds to outline the career of John and the glory of the new world order. John praises God for His fidelity to his people and professes His faith in the future of His Son as a Child of God.

Every parent should be able to shout these powerful words as they lift their child from the baptismal font. At that glorious moment they praise God for blessing their love in the flesh and blood (the Incarnation) of their child. This child will always be a sign of the mercy and goodness of God

45

for making their love fruitful and blessing the Church with a child who will be "prophet of the most high."

This child of theirs will be a light in the darkness because their love will shine through their child with a brilliance and a power that the darkness will never be able to conquer. Their child like Zechariah and Elizabeth's, is hope and promise to a world yearning for love and tenderness. The birth of your child — every child — is the guarantee that there is a God and that there will always be a tomorrow. As you hold your children, praise and glorify God in the words and Spirit of Zechariah and pray "that they will serve Him devoutly and be holy in His sight."

A Dialogue with Santa

(For use at the Christmas Eve Family Masses)

At the time of the Gospel the priest invites all the children into the sanctuary. The congregation is also seated. The celebrant is seated in a chair and there is an empty chair facing him. He then reads Luke's Gospel for Midnight Mass. At the conclusion of the Gospel (Luke 2:15-20) there is a knock:

Priest: Oh my, I wonder who that could be (*Santa pokes his head in*). Why boys and girls, look who's here! Why it's Santa! Hello Santa, Merry Christmas! Welcome to our Mass in honor of Jesus' birth! (*Santa finds his seat facing the priest. He's carrying a package in a little shopping bag.*)

Santa: Father _____, boys and girls, hello and Merry Christmas. I'm so glad to be with you at Mass on this Christmas Eve. I always go to Mass before I make my long and wonderful Christmas Eve journey.

Priest: Santa, each Christmas you make this long journey to the homes of all the boys and girls of the world. Why do you do this each year?

Santa: Well, Father, two thousand years ago in the town of Bethlehem, Jesus the Prince of Peace was born. His birth was the most wonderful thing that ever happened. God came to us as a little baby. The angels sang and everyone was happy.

Priest: Did anyone bring this poor Baby Jesus any gifts?

Santa: Oh, yes. The shepherds brought him fruits and nuts and a baby lamb and the wise persons came and they gave him gold, frankincense and myrrh. I bring gifts to all these beautiful boys and girls to continue the celebration of the Christ Child's birth and to remind the world that *every child* is the Christ Child and *every child* must be loved as we love Jesus.

Priest: What do you think about as you bring the boys and girls their gifts?

Santa: Well, Father, I just pray that these beautiful children will share their gifts with one another — that they will learn to play without fighting — that they will learn to play with everybody and that they will always help those people who are in need.

Priest: Yes, Santa, that's why Jesus came: to teach us how to respect and love all people so that our boys and girls can build the kingdom of God as they love one another.

Santa: Well, Father, I want to give all my girls and boys here a special gift for Christmas. (*Santa gives the package to the priest. He takes out the figurine of Santa praying before the Baby Jesus and holds it up for all to see.*)

Priest: Santa, thank you so much! God bless you and have a wonderful trip. I hope you enjoy the cookies and milk we will all leave for you tonight! (*Santa gets up, waves and says good-bye.*)

All: Good-bye, Santa, Good-bye and thank you!!

Proper Readings of Christmastide

JESUS CHRIST IS BORN! All creation rejoices at this Word that has come to pass. The time of Advent and Christmas proclaims, celebrates and marvels at the mystery of all mysteries — God becoming one of us. The Incarnation — the taking of flesh by the Word of God — His only Son — is the very heart and substance of all Christianity.

As we Christians celebrate that God is "one with us," we celebrate the love beyond all understanding. God loves us so much that He chooses not only to *walk* among us, but to *be* one of us. In Jesus Christ, God and humanity are united in a bond of love that can never be broken. God has entered every phase and part of human life and destiny. He truly is "bone of our bone" and "flesh of our flesh." Our God is no longer only the God of Sinai, the transcendent One, the distant One. Now He is the vulnerable One — the Babe. He is the Little One suckled at the breast of Mary. He is the Poor One born into the world and leaving this world with nothing. He is the Weak One torn apart by doubt and fear and pain in the Garden and on the Cross. He is the Human One weeping at the death of His friend Lazarus.

In Jesus our humanity is recreated and exalted. Jesus blesses and affirms everything in us that is good. Our bodies are declared holy and beautiful again as God recreates us in Jesus and sees that we are indeed *very* good. In Jesus we rediscover that power and the beauty of our emotions, our feelings, our yearnings and our sexuality.

Jesus in His humanity glorifies our need to love and be loved. He shows us how to love deeply, not counting the cost. He teaches us how to be friends. He blesses the marriage bed and consecrates the sexual loving union of husband and wife as a sacrament of His passion and love for us. As husband and wife grow in love, they come to know that as they touch and embrace and love each other, they do so to Christ. The ecstasy of married love becomes a foretaste of the passionate embrace between God and Her/His Lover.

In the power and the glory of Christ's humanity, we look upon His world and creation as friend, not enemy and we see our call as using all things to give glory to the God of Creation and Re-creation in Christ Jesus the Lord. He *is* one of us. Creation can never go back to what it was before Him and neither can we. To believe in Christmas is to believe that there is a new world and that all things have been made new in Jesus Christ — especially you and me.

Christmas Day
Luke 2:1–14

On this holy day let us go even unto Bethlehem to see this event that has taken place. And so, each of us do go to Bethlehem. We enter into the stable/cave of our own hearts to see this wondrous event! God is among us as a little baby.

When we enter a place where animals are kept there is a special smell. Some are offended by it, but others sense it as something very natural —almost healthy. We are deeply moved by it, because in the hay the little baby is placed and the little baby sleeps. We see the holy Mother asleep after giving birth and we see in Mary's face the face of all women who bring life into this world. Mary tells all women what a blessing *they* are as they give life to this world. What seems to be so ordinary is in reality the most extraordinary and the most divine of all things —to have a baby.

The baby stirs and Joseph picks up the child. He will love and protect this child and teach Him how to be a man and how to earn an honest living. He looks into the child's face and sees the faces of all the children of the world. He sees humanity and a world where this child and all children will be loved and He prays for a world without war and violence. Joseph looks at the child in his arms and begins to weep gently. He thinks to himself that "this child will be called the Son of Joseph the carpenter." He smiles with a father's pride.

The baby begins to fuss. He's hungry. So Joseph gently wakes Mary and she places her son at her breast and He begins to feast on the love and security that is mother's milk. This little place in God's world is the whole world. Nothing more holy or sacred can ever take place than when a mother nurses her baby. This is the First Eucharist of humanity —offered by the Mother-Priest. Mary, may we all drink deeply this Christmas of the milk of your son's love. Don't hurry out of the cave. Stay there. Look. Smell. Listen. Speak. Pray for the grace to recognize the birth of Christ taking place around you every day.

> *"Child of Bethlehem, House of Bread,*
> *may we become bread for one another."*

Feast of St. Stephen — December 26
Acts 6:8–10; 7:54–59; Psalm 31:3–4, 6, 7, 8, 17, 21;
Matthew 10:17–22

"Now Stephen, filled with grace and power, was working great wonders and signs among the people."

It doesn't take long for us to realize what it might mean to accept this Child as one's Lord: Stephen is stoned to death. From the very first shedding of the blood of the Holy Innocents to our own day, many have had to shed their blood for believing in Jesus Christ.

Oscar Romero, the Church women and the Jesuits of El Salvador, the tens of thousands of campesinos — all shed their blood and gave their lives because they not only believed that the Prince of Peace was born in Bethlehem, but also tried to bring his dream into their personal lives and the lives of others.

It is fascinating to think about what these saints were doing when they were martyred. Romero was saying Mass (I've done that thousands of times). The sisters were driving home from a meeting. (We've all been to a few of them!) The Jesuits were sleeping. (Everybody does that!) They were all engaged in the most ordinary, mundane — you might say, boring — things possible when the Lord called them home and they gave to Him the gift of their lives.

Their real gift of love (martyrdom) was not the fact that they were murdered at a certain place and time. Their real gift to the Lord was the fidelity of going to the meetings, and saying Mass, and teaching the classes, and going to work, and changing the baby, and doing all the millions of boring, ordinary, dull and seemingly unimportant things with loving hearts and deep fidelity. That's *all* the saints did — day in and day out. And that's what we're doing. And you can't do much better than that. Pray for us, St. Stephen, to say "yes" and to love every moment, and to do the ordinary with extraordinary love.

Feast of St. John the Evangelist — December 27
1 John 1:1–4; Psalm 97:1–2, 5–6, 11–12;
John 20:2–8

In today's Gospel, St. John is referred to as the other disciple (the one Jesus loved) — the one who rested his head on Jesus' breast at the Last Supper. It is interesting to see how uncomfortable people have been with Jesus having "favorites." Yet, it is so clear that Jesus was most comfortable with John, Mary, Martha, Lazarus and Mary Magdalene. He *obviously* loved them. The reaction of Jesus on finding out about the death of Lazarus is exactly what we would expect from the "most human" of us. He wept. There were no pious platitudes like, "this is God's will," or, "how good it is for Lazarus to be with God." None of that. Jesus weeps because he is so upset and the people comment how much He must have loved Lazarus.

Jesus had friends. Jesus had real personal relationships. These relationships were two-way streets. Jesus didn't just summon people to the honor of being His friend. There was a chemistry, an attraction, a "rightness," a communication when He was with them. It grew and it clicked and it had to be nourished or it would die. There were some people Jesus didn't like and there were others who didn't like Him. One can't program friendship or falling in love. It happens. It's part of the joy and the pain of humanity.

Jesus seemed to value friendship very highly. He yearned for its support in the Garden and was denied it. He sought it at the Last Supper — "I call you my friends." Jesus worked at his friendships. He didn't take them for granted. This Christmas season is a good time to examine our friendships. Are you a good friend? Are you a friend of convenience or one of commitment? Our friendships are a very accurate measure of the quality of our relationship with the Lord. They are both capable of purification and growth. In this holy time Jesus reminds us that as we grow in love with one another, we grow in love with Him.

Feast of the Holy Innocents — December 28
1 John 1:5–2:2; Psalm 124:2–3, 4–5, 7–8;
Matthew 2:13–18

In today's Gospel, we relive a scene that is constantly happening all over the world. "Take the Child and His Mother and flee...." How many millions of parents have heard these terrible words! Jesus the Savior identifies with these vast throngs of the poor, the refugees, the aliens, the undocumented, the stranger, and the unwanted. Jesus is one with the homeless, the street people and the disposable ones that no one cares about. Mary and Joseph and the Child are on the road with no safe destination in sight and they're there with the millions who still don't have a home and must wander.

The evil of a Herod murdering children is still being lived out in our world. On this day we pray for an end to abortion, while we lovingly embrace our sisters and brothers who have had abortions and reassure them of the loving mercy of Jesus who embraces them, loves them and tells them "I forgive." But let us all ask for forgiveness for the abortions of the poor who see no way out of the poverty their children will be condemned to if they are born. Let us repent of the conditions of poverty and desperation that are allowed to exist. Let's also repent of the horror of so many children who go to bed hungry each night or who are the victims of abuse, war and murder. Let's hold in our arms and hearts the many who are not loved or cherished as they should be.

We are a pro-life Church. We seek peace and justice for all. We condemn violence, war, killing, the death penalty, abortion, poverty, ignorance and inhumanity in any form. We choose life — the ultimate and eternal value of all life — born and unborn. May all the Holy Innocents of all ages pray and forgive us — for we *know* what we are doing. May their prayer move us to create a new world of love, peace and justice — especially for children.

Feast of St. Thomas Becket — December 29
Wisdom 3:1–9; James:2–4, 12;
John 12:24–26

Still another Christmas martyr! This martyrdom is set in the dynamics of a great friendship, that of King Henry II of England and his chancellor, Thomas Becket, whom he made Archbishop of Canterbury. Becket will be murdered by agents of his King in Canterbury Cathedral in 1170. It's always a great treat to watch the film *Becket* and see the story unfold. Romero and Becket share a common fate. They love the Lord and His people more than any prince of this world. They both fall at the assassin's hand at the Lord's table.

Henry appoints his friend archbishop because he wants to control the Church. It's one of the ugliest examples of corruption and perversion, not only in the state, but in the Church. Money can buy anything, even an archbishopric! But something happens to Becket — he comes to realize who he is and in that realization everything changes.

Christmas is a beautiful season for us to realize who *we* are and to begin to live accordingly. We are all very special. We are called to be His followers by living out as faithfully and as lovingly as we can *our* role and *our* vocation. Mother, father, friend, sister, brother, priest, deacon, teacher — each of these titles spell out a whole life of commitment, service and love.

Each of us know exactly what the Lord is calling us to be or to do. Ultimately, it will be to love with all we've got to the point of laying down our life in love for our little flock. We are all called to be the good shepherd —living for and dying for someone else —and in that process gaining eternal life.

5th & 6th Days of Octave —December 29 & 30
1 John 2:3–17; Psalm 96:1–2, 2–3, 5–6;
Luke 2:22–40

In Luke's Gospel for today and yesterday, we see the touching scene of Mary and Joseph bringing the Child Jesus to the Temple for the Presentation and Purification rituals. The prophesies of Simeon and Anna speak movingly of this child who comes to bring salvation and life to all people.

It is so touching to see this young couple who want to do everything "right" for their child. They live in our parishes and are still trying to do what's "right" for their children.

At the birth of a child, God enters the life experience of a couple in a powerful, dramatic and moving manner. It is *the* most religious event of their lives. To hold one's child is to be part of the miracle of creation. As the couple prepares for baptism it is a special moment for the Church to affirm the holiness and the grace of this moment in their lives. The Church calls them to recognize what they already possess — holiness. That holiness is *being* wife and husband, mother and father.

The experience of the birth of their child and the raising of that child to know and to love the Lord Jesus is their sacred and divine call to continue the loving presence of Jesus in this world. God can give them no greater grace than to live the sacrament of marriage and parenthood. Each week at Eucharist the Church will celebrate the ritual of "reminding" — telling Her beloved people — *who* they are and *what* they already possess — *everything*. There is really nothing more that the Church has to give them.

The Church will remind them that family life is the living Church and that life itself is the Holy Eucharist celebrated at the Altar of the Family. In this holy season, the Church cannot stop telling us that we already have everything. We have to recognize it, claim it and live it.

New Year's Eve — December 31
1 John 2:18–21; Psalm 96:1–2, 11–12, 13;
John 1:1–18

Today we read the beginning of St. John's Gospel — those majestic words: "In the beginning was the Word, . . ." This Gospel of Incarnation and the coming of the Christ doesn't deal with the tender scene of Bethlehem and the shepherds but with the philosophical meaning of the birth of the Lord.

John refers to Jesus as the light. The light shines in the darkness and the darkness has never been able to put it out. New Year's Eve is a good day to pray over the events in our lives — the joys and the sorrows.

Christ has loved us so much that He has *always* been with us. He has *never* abandoned us. He has *never* let anything put out the light of faith and love. Our Lord has used everything in our experience to bring us closer to Him — even our sins. He has guided us and protected us through all the struggles and all the deaths we have had to endure. And the Light has never gone out. Darkness was never stronger than the love we have experienced in Christ Jesus Our Lord.

This day is one of gratitude for what *has* been and one of expectation for what *will* be — He has never given up on us and He never will. He loves us insanely. We can't fully comprehend that kind of love, yet that is what it means to have Jesus as Savior. In great peace let us give Him what has been and embrace what He has in store for us.

Happy New Year!

Solemnity of Mary, Mother of God — January 1
World Day of Peace
Numbers 6:22–27; Psalm 67:2–3, 5, 6, 8; Galatians 4:4–7
Luke 2:16–21

In the Gospel today we are told that Mary held in her heart all the events of the birth of her beloved son. Mary, like every mother, cherished every detail of the growth of her beloved child. Mary also feared for the very life of her son as his life was threatened by forces of hate and violence. This same mother would someday hold the lifeless body of her beloved son under the cross of His execution.

On this day of world peace Mary is one with all the mothers of the world — the sorrowful mothers who cherish their children as she did, but who fear for their very existence. Mary is the mother in the war torn areas of this world where children are the daily victims of the paranoia and hate of politicians. Mary is one with mothers living in poverty and watching their children suffering from hunger and lack of decent housing. Mary is the welfare mother suffering more and more from an indifferent society and governments interested more in balanced budgets than the lives of children.

Mary is the sorrowful mother watching the new slaughter of the innocents in the holocaust of abortion. She is the mother who is sometimes driven to this desperate step by the lack of love and support of our society. Mary is also the sorrowful mother who has had an abortion and so much needs the healing mercy and compassion of the Church to begin a new life.

Feast of the Holy Family
Sunday in the Octave of Christmas
Matthew 2:13–15, 19–23; Luke 2:22–40; Luke 2:41–52
The All Too Holy Families

A feast that brings great joy for many of us is the Feast of the Holy Family. In the liturgy, sacred art, music and always in sermons, Jesus, Mary, and Joseph are held up to us as the model of what a family should be. Certainly, their love for each other is an ideal that all of our families work to achieve. While the Church constantly encourages her people, especially in Pre-Cana, Baptism Prep Programs and Family Life Ministry, to become that loving union of husband and wife and children, many of our very holy families don't fit into the mold of the Holy Family we find in Scripture.

Today, many of our families are shepherded by a single parent. These families possess as much love, tenderness and commitment as the "ideal" family, in fact sometimes they are more of a family than the "ideal." It is very important that the single parent know that he/she is not a second-class citizen of the Church and that their family is just as precious and important to the Body of Christ as the "Perfect American Family." The Church — translated you and I — has the difficult but necessary task of teaching and preaching that "ideal," while at the same time making *all* feel loved, wanted, appreciated and just as important as the "PAF."

The single person is for the most part an afterthought in what the Church teaches and celebrates as family. But the single person is part of family, too. The single person lives out relationships of love and commitment to many people. Their special ways of being family must be explained and understood better by the Church.

Not everyone will or should marry. The unmarried are just as significant as those who marry and raise a family. They must be inspired and challenged always to build bonds of family, friendship and love. They obviously have something very important to share with the family of the Church. Let's not forget that much of what is spoken or written about Family Life is done so by people who are *not* married — your celibate clergy and nuns being the prime example of that group. We single people *do* have something to offer.

The Church and society today are grappling with family structures and groupings the world has never had to face before. Divorce, widowhood, out-of-wedlock birth, single parenthood, unhappy marriages, single life, homosexual couples, etc., etc. — the list gets longer each year. In it all, Christ is present calling His disciples to love one another as He has first loved us. He calls us to respect and esteem each other, even when we don't agree with another's lifestyle. Always, He calls us to create a Church where everyone belongs and has a place.

Celebrating this Feast of the Holy Family becomes more difficult each year. The holy card depiction of the Holy Family doesn't really work any more. No family is like that and probably never was. The holy families today work very hard. Many live in real evangelical poverty to be able to survive and to give their children what they need. The *real* holy family today prays a lot about what it should do and be. Loving is a joy and a gift, but it is also struggle, pain, self-denial and ultimately laying down one's life for the beloved.

There are many people living that way today. They don't know it, but they are the saints of today's Church. They are the holy families of today. These real saints make a commitment and try their absolute best to live it out. They love with all their hearts and give it everything they've got. But sometimes, it doesn't work out and they have to pick up the pieces and start over again. That's *really* being a saint!

Feast of the Epiphany — January 6

Isaiah 60:1–6; Ps. 72:1–2, 7–8, 12–13; Ephesians 3:2–3, 5–6;
Matthew 2:1–12

Everyone loves this exotic feast! What little boy hasn't wished to be picked as one of the Three Kings in the Christmas pageant? The crowns, the robes, the gold, frankincense and myrrh are all irresistible to the child and even the children at heart. Yet, the levels of meaning and interpretation of this Gospel are very complex and are filled with spiritual nourishment and challenges. As we celebrate this feast let's try to interpret the meaning of the three gifts for the Christ Child for our own children today. In so doing, we will see that parents continue to bring the gifts to Christ as they give them to their children.

The *gold* symbolizes the human needs of the Christ Child and also His Kingship. Parents continue to bring that gift of gold to the Christ Child as they care for the physical and material needs of their children. The labor and work that parents expend to care for the material needs of a family are holy and sacramental. Their work must always be esteemed and appreciated by the Church. Work at home or out of the home is the love of parents expressed in action. We should never think of our work here as less than spiritual or holy. Sometimes we completely underestimate or totally misunderstand the sacramental power of work and commuting, overtime and business trips, second or third jobs, shopping and driving the kids to CCD, etc. All of these labors are precious in the eyes of the Lord as parents try so hard to care for their family. Of course, our prayer life will guide us so that we do not become obsessed by the material or forget that everything is meant for the glory of the Lord and the service of His Body, the Church. We are truly becoming one with the Lord when our work *is* our prayer.

The *frankincense* symbolizes the divinity of the Child and is a sign of the worship of the Kings. Parents continue to bring that gift of frankincense to the Christ Child as they nurture the spiritual growth of their children. After their child has been baptized, the Church gives the child back to his/her parents with the challenge to bring their baby home to the "little church" — their home — to complete what was begun at baptism. Parents will be priest to their children as they preach the Gospel by the example of their love and their lives. Family life and meals will be a continuous celebration of the Eucharist of Life. Nothing can ever do more to form these children than for them to live in a loving faith-filled home. Family traditions like setting up the Nativity scene, observing Advent and Christmas, Lent and Easter and Pentecost — all this is how the faith life of their divine children will grow and blossom until the day comes when they will say, "I believe." If parents don't do their job of forming their sons and daughters in the image of the divine child, who will do it?

The *myrrh* is used to anoint a corpse in preparation for burial. There is already cast upon the stable of Bethlehem the shadow of the cross. The divine child must follow his destiny to the cross and eventually to glory. Parents continue to bring that gift of myrrh to the Christ child as they teach their children that as beautiful and wonderful as this world is, there is another. Parents bring the myrrh to their children as they teach them the real meaning of love and how one must lay down one's life in love for the beloved — just as Jesus did for the world and just as they do for one another and for their children. The myrrh will remind their children that they must enter into the power of the Paschal mystery and as they put to death in their own hearts hatred, envy, evil thoughts, selfishness, etc. a new life arrives — the life of the Kingdom in the Holy Spirit.

This Epiphany, as parents give their spiritual gifts to their children, they will be reminded that their true life and holiness will consist in generously and continuously giving these gifts to their children. As they look upon the faces of their children they will see the face of Jesus and they will know that the exhaustion, sleepless nights, tight budgets, lack of personal time and all the sacrificing they do each and every day are all worth it, because all these things worship the Child and in them is their peace and joy.

The Baptism of Jesus — Sunday after January 6
Matthew 3:13–17; Mark 1:7–11; Luke 3:15–16, 21–22

On this beautiful day, the Christmas Season comes to an end. We have walked with Mary through the touching and moving days of her pregnancy. We have yearned with Israel of old for the coming of the Messiah and we have celebrated the Lord's birth at Bethlehem. Every day as we have read and prayed over the scriptures we have been anointed by the Holy Spirit to understand another aspect of the Lord's personal and redeeming love for us.

Today at the River Jordan the ministry of Jesus and our own ministry begins. The Father speaks the words of consecration over Jesus and over each of us. In Matthew, Mark and Luke, we hear the Father say: "This is my beloved Son (Daughter) upon whom my favor rests."

Each of us must know that the Father *does* speak these words of anointing over each of us. We *are* His beloved son or daughter. His favor and blessing *does* rest upon us. We have tried to truly celebrate the savior's birth. We have invited Him into our hearts. We have given Him our sins and brokenness and we are certain of His complete and total forgiveness. We have embraced Him as our Lord and savior. The process of our transformation is not complete yet. But when a son or daughter truly wishes to live the new and abundant life and truly accepts Jesus as Lord and begins the journey, then the Father sings a song of joy declaring us to be His beloved children upon whom His pleasure, love and favor rest forever.

This favor of the Father that we experience does not mean

that we're perfect or that we will never fall or make mistakes again. It means that we're on the right road and that all we have to do when we stumble is to take His hand and let Him draw us to Himself again.

We are His precious and beautiful saints. But what is a saint? Someone who is perfect and has never sinned? No! *A saint is a* sinner *who never gives up*. Remember, each saint has a past and every sinner has a future with Jesus. This holy season has again reminded us of the promise of the Father's Love for us incarnate in the Child of Bethlehem. Now we continue the Incarnation as we are the flesh and blood of Jesus Christ to one another. In our love and fidelity Christmas will last forever.

Special Days of Advent and Christmastide

Joseph Cardinal Bernardin of Chicago — November 14

On November 14, 1996 the tears of grief and love of millions of Americans of every faith, color and nationality declared Joseph Bernardin a saint. We had all lost a father, a brother and a friend. The Church in the United States was so proud of this holy bishop who was truly a good shepherd to all of us and a role model to every bishop, priest, religious and lay minister. Joseph Bernardin taught us how to live and how to die. It was fairness, integrity, truthfulness, forgiveness and, of course, love, that permeated his life.

The last thing that Joseph Bernardin wrote as he prepared for death was *The Gift of Peace*. This book is a magnificent meditation for these days leading up to Christmas. They speak so powerfully of his struggle to open his heart and his life to Christ. This is what Advent is all about: opening our hearts so that the Prince of Peace may enter in and reign as King.

The opening section of his book is entitled: "Letting Go." Much of the book will develop that theme — how he spent his life "letting go" so that the Lord might enter in. His honest confession of what "letting go" meant as he learned how to pray, administer a huge archdiocese (without compromising his integrity), faced false sexual abuse accusations and finally learned to embrace pancreatic cancer and his "friend" death, challenges us as we look forward to another Advent to "let go" of all the extra baggage we carry through our lives.

Joseph Cardinal Bernardin was a teacher. He taught through the gift of his intellect. His exposition of the "seamless garment" will stand perhaps as the greatest statement of the Church's stand for life in all its stages. He taught us that no one can pull out a single thread of the garment. All the threads, all the parts of the Gospel of Life, must be preserved or the seamless garment will unravel and be no more. To be "pro-life" one must embrace all issues of life. The Catholic must be against violence, murder, war, abortion, euthanasia, assisted suicide, racism, prejudice, poverty, malnutrition, illiteracy, homelessness, sexism, homophobia, abuse of children, slavery. All of these life issues are part of his brilliant teaching on the holiness and sacredness of all life expressed in the image of the seamless garment.

It is absolute absurdity to be against abortion but be in favor of government budgets that leave children hungry, homeless or poorly educated. It is just as absurd to be against hand guns and the death penalty and to support partial birth abortion as a "choice" of a mother. If we are not for all life, we are for none because we are choosing who will live and who will die.

More than by his words Joseph Bernardin taught by his life. His charity, forgiveness, largeness of spirit, tolerance and compassion made him stand out as a beacon of what a priest and Christian should be. He was loved because his life was that of the humble shepherd who laid down his life for his little flock each and every day of his life. He was everybody's bishop because he loved everyone and saw himself as everyone's brother.

In his dying, Brother Joseph showed how to live. In his dying he became even more pastorally involved as he reached out to his fellow cancer patients. He was able to become what Fr. Damien was years ago to the lepers of Molakai when he said: "we lepers." He could say: "we cancer patients." There is no home in the whole United States that has not suffered a death from cancer. Our brother Joseph knew what he was talking about as he helped patients, families and caregivers find the gift of peace that he himself found as he finally "let go" and allowed the Lord to enter in.

May Joseph's loving presence inspire each of us this Advent to "let go" so that we may find the gift of peace. Brother Joseph, thank you for your beautiful life and your loving death.

The Jesuit Martyrs of the Central American University — November 16

Early in the morning of November 16, 1989 Fathers Ignacio Ellacuria, Segundo Montes, Juan Ramon Moreno, Joaquin Lopez y Lopez, Ignacio Martin-Baro, Amando Lopez and their housekeeper, Elba Ramos, and her daughter Celina Ramos were roused from their sleep, taken to the garden of the Jesuit residence and shot to death.

The brains of the Jesuits were blown out of their skulls — as if by this horrible act the forces of evil could stop or destroy the spirit of their minds, intellects and souls. These holy men who had given their lives to the people of El Salvador by challenging their nation to think and reason and to wage peace by securing the rights of the people, especially the poor, were massacred like animals. Their murderers thought they could stop an idea or movement by destroying the teachers, reconcilers, priests and servants of the people who gave their whole lives to live justice, peace, and love.

How wrong the barbarians always are! One can never suppress the truth. It always rises like the phoenix from the ashes to convict and judge the people of the lie. The Jesuits of El Salvador spoke their final and eternal word of truth as they shed their blood for their flock whom they had faithfully served as servants of the truth. Their witness will live forever inspiring the youth of their country to always seek after and live the truth.

Institutions, including the Church, find it very difficult, if not impossible, to say: "We were wrong" and "we are sorry — we repent." Our own Church has still not totally embraced the guilt and shame we share with our country for the Holocaust. We still haven't accepted the blame for creating the need for the Reformation. We are *not* seen as the Church that always espouses truth and justice, no matter what. We are often perceived as just the opposite. We are often perceived as underhanded, politically wheeling and dealing, deceptive and more the enemy than the defender of the truth. Thank God for the people of faith like the Salvadoran Jesuits who show us the true face of the Church — the defender of truth and justice — even to the laying down of one's life.

As these holy martyrs lead us into Advent, perhaps their greatest gift to us is to remind us how important, even essential, the truth is in the life of the Christian. Our light should shine before all people, never fearing the light or finding solace in the darkness because we speak and live the truth from the mountain tops. To know and live the truth is to be set free and to lead others to freedom.

May the blood of these men and women water the soil of El Salvador to bring forth a new harvest of truth and freedom to a country that has suffered martyrdom again and again. May we all give up duplicity, lies, politics, underhandedness and half truths and always live in the splendor of the brightness of truth. Surely, that is why Christ comes to live among us. Surely, that is the real and true meaning of Christmas.

Dorothy Day of New York — November 29
Proverbs 31:10–31; **Matthew 25:31–46**

Dorothy Day! Saint? Well, the Church hasn't formally canonized her yet, but there are tens of thousands she fed, clothed, sheltered, loved and served who shout up to heaven: "Thank you, Dorothy, pray for us!"

Pray for us indeed! Pray for us who find ways of diluting the radical power of the Gospel we twist to serve our own convenience and who create a respectable version of Jesus who is always clean, well-groomed and definitely acceptable in our churches.

This was *not* the Jesus of Dorothy Day. The Jesus she loved and served was the unkempt and stinking derelict. He was the alcoholic, the addict, the homeless person. Dorothy saw Jesus in the face of the frightened and hungry children.

Dorothy revolutionized the Catholic Church in the United States. She inspired countless priests, seminarians, sisters and lay people to pick up the scriptures and believe in the revolution Jesus is trying to accomplish. Jesus is calling the world to live as children of God in pacifism and nonviolence and to share all our possessions with one another. Jesus is interested in a new world in which there is no war or violence — living as His family, serving, helping and sharing with one another.

Dorothy, like Jesus, was an idealistic fool. How can love, gentleness, kindness and mercy ever survive in a world filled with hate, suspicion, violence and greed? People like Dorothy and her Jesus have to learn that it is money that really talks! They have to learn never to trust again or forgive anyone who has stabbed you in the back or hurt you. Ultimately, it *is* an eye for an eye and a tooth for a tooth. Be careful. Don't let your guard down. Take care of yourself.

But the great fool Jesus and all his crazy friends like Dorothy, Francis of Assisi, John XXIII, Mother Teresa, etc., continue to pop up through the ages to amaze and antagonize us and make us feel guilty. They really *do* turn the other cheek. They really *do* forgive seventy times seven. They are very dangerous people to have in a Church! They have that annoying habit of opening the New Testament to chapter 25 in Matthew, and saying to us with a twinkle in their eye: "Read it, honey! It's true!"

St. Andrew of Bethsaida and Scotland —
November 30
John 1:29–42

Whether Andrew ever made it to Scotland we don't know. Our Scottish sisters and brothers will swear that he did and they have a flag to prove it. Frankly, if Andrew had heard of the Scot's great whiskey I'm sure he would have made the journey. Wouldn't you have? Nothing beats a St. Andrew's Rob Roy!

In the Gospel of John we see that Andrew is present as John the Baptist points to Jesus and says: "Behold the Lamb of God." Andrew and Peter follow Jesus that day and become His disciples. They will be with Him for keeps.

St. Andrew is the one who introduces us to Advent. The First Sunday of Advent is the Sunday closest to Andrew's feast day. Andrew begins that wonderful ragtag group who through the ages have left father, mother, husband, wife, property — everything to follow Jesus. The beautiful Gospel speaks about our vocation and call.

Today, men and women still hear that call in their hearts and have no choice but to embrace Jesus and follow Him. The following of Jesus is a strong and burning desire to love Him above all others and to serve Him in His sisters and brothers, especially the poor. This call continues to be present in our world even though less seem to be hearing it today.

As we pray for religious vocations we must pray for those who are living vocations in the Church today, that they be signs of radical love and dedication that vocations are meant to be. If our clergy and religious lack the spark of passion and joy in the Lord's service, who would want to be like them? Young people do not want to give themselves to bourgeois mediocrity, they want to embrace passionate and reckless giving of oneself to the Cause and Master.

The magnificent vocations of Christian love: priesthood, religious life, marriage, single life and the diaconate need passionate, happy, dedicated role models who get a kick out of what they're doing and are unmistakably happy in who they are and what they do.

The spirit of Andrew will continue as we really live our vocations and not just play at them.

The Martyrs of El Salvador — December 2
Maura Clarke, Ita Ford, Jean Donovan
and Dorothy Kazel
John 12:20–27

In their wildest dreams Maura Clarke, Ita Ford, Jean Donovan and Dorothy Kazel could never have pictured themselves as a modern-day Agnes, Cecilia or Joan of Arc. The notion of martyrdom was beyond their wildest dreams. When their generation went through formation there was a strong orientation toward service and seeing and finding Jesus in others. They were typical products of Vatican II spirituality in their openness to the world and their belief that they would receive far more from the people they served than they could ever give.

The injustice in El Salvador would escalate and become so evil and terrible that one could look upon that tortured land as the Kingdom of Evil where tens of thousands of El Salvadoran sons and daughters would wash its soil with their blood. Among the martyred would be numbered Archbishop Oscar Romero, the Jesuits and their household, and these holy women — the nuns Maura, Dorothy, Ita and the lay minister, Jean. One night they were coming home from a meeting and they were ambushed, raped and brutally murdered —executed for their work with and for the poor of that troubled land.

I am deeply moved not just by their martyrdom but what led up to it. Martyrdom was the culmination of lives of love and total giving that they had lived day in and day out as servants of the Lord and of his people.

The symbol of the "meeting" is so powerful. Countless servants of the Lord sit for hours at meetings that are usually boring and tiresome. We do so because the community *can* do so much more than any individual. Building community is hard; working as one is even harder. Yet, the servants of the Lord keep on trying to make one little area of the world a little bit holier and happier. What a miracle of love and martyrdom that we don't give up but keep on trying. Long before the bullets ripped through their bodies on that terrible day, Maura, Ita, Jean and Dorothy had given their lives to the Lord. Their lives were a witness of love —of martyrdom — as they gave themselves in love each day in the countless seemingly insignificant things.

As we remember these holy saints today, let us remember that we are doing in our daily lives what they did in their daily lives. Meetings, deadlines, projects, classes, caring for children, building relationships —all of it is our daily witness of love — our martyrdom. It is all so holy and so precious to Jesus.

"I hope you find that which gives life a deep meaning for you. Something worth living for... maybe even worth dying for... something that energizes you, enthuses you and enables you to keep moving ahead."

—Ita Ford

St. Francis Xavier — December 3
1 Corinthians 9:16–19; **Mark 16:15–21**

Francis Xavier was the first of the big fish landed by the great Ignatius Loyola. In true missionary zeal he badgered Francis, the worldly libertine at the University of Paris, with the question: "What does it profit a man to gain the whole world and lose his soul in the process?" Thomas More used the same question to put Richard Rich in his place after Richard's perjury condemned Thomas to death. He quoted the scripture with the addendum: "But for Wales?"

Francis eventually heard the challenge and was converted, becoming one of the first Jesuits. There's nothing like the conversion of a first-class sinner! They redirect all that negative energy into Holy Spirit energy and change the world in the process. The fruits of the conversion of Francis had tremendous ramifications in the life of the Church.

Francis became so consumed with his new love and with Jesuit spirituality that he went to India as a missionary. The vitality of the faith of millions of Indian people today traces its roots back to this Spanish Basque who had to finally tell Ignatius — to get him off his back — that he would follow him as a Jesuit and begin a new life.

The season of Advent and the feast of Francis Xavier invite us to look at our personal conversion. Are we going through the motions of the Christian life or have we embraced the Living Jesus with all the passion and love in our hearts? Francis asks us the same question that Ignatius asked him, "What does it profit...?" Thomas More throws in his, "but for Wales," just to complete the picture. What is *your* Wales? What is more important to you than the love of Jesus?

The Feast of St. Nicholas — December 6

The Feast of St. Nicholas reminds us of what's on the minds of children during Advent — Santa Claus and gifts and toys. It also brings us face to face with the conflict between spirituality and commercialism or Jesus versus Santa. Indeed, we have come to a point where Christmas has been reduced to a secular winter festival. "Merry Christmas" has been replaced by "Have a nice holiday." What is the Christian parent to do with the wonder of a child waiting for Santa's visit and the desire we have to share our faith in Jesus born in Bethlehem?

First of all, let's claim our roots: Santa is our own Saint Nicholas. At the heart of all the legends about St. Nicholas is his love of the poor and his love of children. Santa Claus develops as a continuation of the ministry of the good Bishop-Saint. There is so much good and beauty in the Santa figure. Santa (Nicholas) was even present at the first Ecumenical Council in Nicea in 325 AD!

At our Christmas Eve Family Masses (see pp. 47–48) the priest gathers the children around him as he reads the Gospel. There is a knock and it is Santa who joins the group. The sermon consists of a dialogue between Santa and the priest. Santa is asked why he visits all the children each Christmas. He responds that it is the birthday of the Lord Jesus and just as the Wise men brought Him gifts many years ago, he continues to give children gifts at Christmas because each child is truly the Christ Child.

Santa goes on to say that as he visits each home he prays that the boys and girls will share their toys with one another and that they will love all the children of the world who are poor. He prays that they will share with the poor by continuing to bring food to church on Sundays. He tells them that they should not be selfish or greedy and that the thing that matters most is that Jesus has come to them again this Christmas.

Before Santa leaves, he gives the priest a gift for all the children of the parish — a figurine of Santa kneeling before the Baby Jesus. The priest accepts the gift, blesses it and places it on the altar for the remainder of the Mass. The cantor then sings the beautiful song: "I Saw Santa Praying At the Baby Jesus' Cradle."

The Church always takes good secular symbols, "baptizes" them, and then uses them to the glory of God. The celebration of Christmas on December 25 is a perfect example. But as important as bringing Santa into the religious dimension he deserves, it is just as important to create the religious atmosphere at home that Advent/Christmas deserve. Parents have to work at not letting their children become too materialistic. Sometimes the waste and lack of self-control of children at Christmas is a reflection of adult materialism. Advent has to be used as a gradual journey to Bethlehem. There are many wonderful Advent calendars that help with this. Families must create their own customs and liturgies. Setting up the crib, decorating the Christmas tree, baking cookies, watching "It's A Wonderful Life," etc. — all of these things will help to make Advent holy in the hearts of our children as the birth of the Baby Jesus draws near.

We don't have to put down Santa. Use him as you do the shepherds and the Wise men at the Crib. Santa is another believer touched by the Son of God, who comes to worship Him and to continue the yearly celebration of His birth until He comes again.

Feast of the Immaculate Conception — December 8
Genesis 3:9–15, 20; Psalm 98:1–4;
Ephesians 1:3–6:11–12; **Luke 1:26–38**

This beautiful feast of Mary is one of the highlights of Advent. The Church celebrates today how Mary was preserved free of original sin at the moment of her conception in the womb of her mother, Anne. Mary is chosen from all women to be the Mother of the Savior.

In today's Gospel we read the beautiful story of the Annunciation as the Angel Gabriel invites Mary to become the Mother of the Lord. Mary freely speaks her "yes." That "yes" transforms all human history as creation begins again in the womb of the Virgin of Nazareth. Mary is the model of the person of faith who places his/her life totally in the hands of God. Ultimately, the Lord is waiting for our "yes." He is waiting for that moment of conversion and total love when we give Him everything. When we have said our "yes" then all the things in our lives make sense and fit in their proper places. Our "yes" makes Jesus the Lord of our lives — the center and cornerstone of our families, our work, our dreams and our hopes.

That "yes" brings us the peace for which we yearn. That "yes" places the Lord where he belongs — at the very center of our hearts. Mary is our model of faith. She says "yes" not fully knowing or understanding where the Lord will lead her. She trusts and she believes. Because of her faith the Messiah and Lord comes into this world, and because we say our "yes" the Lord continues to come into this world which so yearns for healing and love. It is our "yes" to the Lord's call that brings that healing and love today.

Thomas Merton — December 10

Thomas Merton died in 1968 in Bangkok, the victim of a freak electrical accident. In death he continues to fascinate, challenge and inspire literally millions who continue to ponder his 1947 autobiography, *Seven Storey Mountain,* and the many books he wrote in the course of his monastic life.

Thomas Merton, the monk, had an incredible impact upon the literary world through his autobiography. It not only brought a large number of people to investigate and even embrace the Church, but it fired up new interest in monasticism and contemplative prayer. There is no question in many people's minds that Thomas Merton was, and is, the most influential thinker and teacher in the history of the Church in the United States.

In his prolific writing on prayer and the spiritual life, he expressed his knowledge and experience of God in understandable terms. He had the ability to express the inexpressible. He was a mystic, poet, dreamer and man of passionate and diverse emotions.

In Thomas' early days, he was a clerical snob, looking down his nose at the "world." That "world" was an evil, sinful place for our Tom and the monastery was the safe haven, the holy place.

As Thomas matured he began to understand that the world and people are holy and belong to God. He grew to appreciate the beauty of people's lives and struggles. He acquired "the fire in the belly" as he began to understand the evil of war, prejudice and the "Bomb." His conversion was slow but sure. Then he had an experience on March 18, 1958 on the corner of Fourth and Walnut in Louisville, Kentucky, in which he felt a bonding and solidarity with every person as his sister and brother. This experience marked his life forever.

Thomas' life as a monk and writer was to seek and find God — the purpose of every life. He was very faithful to the seeking until the day of his tragic death. In life he sought God faithfully, but probably never completely found the God of peace and love until he opened his eyes in death and saw the face of God.

Perhaps the example of Thomas this Advent will inspire us never to cease seeking Him and perhaps it will challenge us to give up our illusions of thinking that we can contain the God of love in bibles, tabernacles and liturgies. While He *is* there, His presence is not limited to them. Our God is too great ever to be contained. We, like our brother Thomas, are called and challenged to find Him in all things. That is the exploration and journey of our lives. May we never be satisfied with a little God that we can contain and lock up. Thomas, pray for us! May we never cease the journey.

Feast of Our Lady of Guadalupe —December 12
Zechariah 2:14–17; Psalm 45:11–12, 14–17;
Luke 1:26–38 or Luke 1:39–47

The Virgin Mary is pregnant in the picture of Our Lady of Guadalupe found on Juan Diego's tilma. Because of Mary's pregnant depiction she has become the special patroness of the *Right To Life* movement. Mary carrying Jesus is the perfect image of our call to affirm life and humanity. It is unfortunate that so many beautiful and well-meaning Christians seem to latch on to only one part of the consistent ethic of life espoused in the "seamless garment" image of Cardinal Bernardin and neglect or undervalue the other aspects of the ethic of life.

Any Christian seeing the image of Our Lady of Guadalupe is naturally opposed to abortion. The taking of innocent life is repugnant to the Christian. But the Christian must also oppose the conditions of poverty that lead some to consider abortion. The Christian is also opposed to other *Right To Life* issues like being against war and hunger and the death penalty as well as being against prejudice leveled at homosexuals and other groups who are not "in" at the time. The consistent ethic of life leads us to renounce prejudice and racism of all kinds and any cuts in local and state budgets that deprive innocent poor children of the basics of their lives.

The Virgin of Guadalupe reminds us powerfully how terrible abortion is, but she also reminds us that to be truly Catholic, is to be *pro-life* in all its forms. If we are avid supporters of only some of the issues of life, then we lack the true Catholic heart of being for life in all its forms. Let us

78

pray that this Advent all those who espouse life issues will at least *listen* to one another. Unfortunately, one of the greatest scandals of the Church is that beautiful and holy people who espouse different aspects of the life movement do not respect or talk to one another. We cannot be single-issue people — *Catholic means that everyone and all life is sacred.*

St. Lucy — December 13

My mother often warned me of the danger of burning the candle at both ends. I never really got why that was such a bad thing to do. Why not have double the light and double the fun! I still deal with the obsession of getting all the light and life possible out of each moment and each day.

Lucy gives me great encouragement in getting that light and life, but she also leads priests to distraction. As much as we try to "baptize" and "catechize" the bonfires and candles she is celebrated with, Lucy continues to take us back to the pre-Christian days which some like to call "pagan."

Pagan, indeed! Pagans are the country folk, the unsophisticated, the people who live and work, sleep and rise according to the sun. They are in tune with nature, planets, moon, sky, stars, earth and fire. They saw the power and manifestation of God in the elements and they worshipped them. Long before Moses and Isaiah and Jesus himself — men and women — our ancestors were deeply religious. Isn't it sad the "new-pagans" don't see as much of God in his beautiful creation as did our ancestors. Isn't it strange that "religious" can be so taken up with books and sacraments that they fail to experience their God in the prime sacrament of them all — their humanity. Our bodies, sexuality, emotions, feelings, thoughts and desires are all manifestations of the God who dwells within. "God saw that it was good" (Genesis 1). What a tragedy when His people are so taken up with worship and order that they cannot read the book of this wonder in creation!

So good old Lucy, our little Sicilian martyr, is patroness of people with eye trouble. As kids we loved the statues of St. Lucy holding a plate with her eyes on it. (They were poked out because she would not break her vow of virginity. But thank God even with two beautiful blue eyes on a plate, she still had two beautiful eyes in her head!) Lucy is still popular with people as the one to pray to when you have trouble with your eyes.

Lucy, though, is really the saint of the Winter Solstice. Her feast day used to fall on that day — the shortest day of the year. Her feast day with its accompanying lighting of candles and fires reminded everyone that the darkness was over and the sun would be with us brighter and longer each day. The feast of St. Lucy brings us in touch with the earthiness of real liturgy. It is not by mistake or chance that we use bread, wine, water, fire and oil. The Easter Vigil Liturgy (even after the prudes cleaned it up) is still alive with illusions and symbols of fertility, life, fire, oil and beautiful sexuality. Genesis 1 said: "God saw that it was *very* good."

In the darkness of winter we rejoice with Lucy that the sun of God's love and mercy shines upon the earth again. Jesus is born to dispel that darkness. "The light shines in the darkness and the darkness has never been able to put it out" (John 1:5).

I conclude this little piece on St. Lucy with two great recipes from our wonderful rectory cook — Michelina Gambale, a Sicilian of course! Do enjoy your Happy Hour after first having your Holy Hour in the beautiful "Walk of Thanksgiving and Praise" by Sister Thelma Hall, RC. The Walk captures the spirit of the beauty of creation which is so much a part of the gift of St. Lucy.

A Walk of Thanksgiving and Praise

Some of God's richest gifts to us we tend to accept as "standard equipment," somehow rightfully ours as fully equipped human beings. It may prove revelatory to consciously cancel this presumption in an experience we call "A Walk of Thanksgiving and Praise," and rediscover, under the very plenitude of God's goodness to us, the unique gifts of love He has made to us, in each of our five senses."

A walk of about a half hour is suggested. Begin as you would any period of prayer: take a few moments to alert yourself to the gift of union with you which He has bestowed in His loving, living presence, always within you who are a "temple of the Holy Spirit."

As you step outdoors, take a breath of fresh air . . . reflect upon how rarely you advert to it as sustainer of your life, day and night, the unceasing providence of God whose love holds you in existence, and is continually creating you.

When you have walked far enough to be out of earshot of anyone, pause *to consciously experience* the use of your

SIGHT . . . use your vision to revel in, caress, enjoy, discern: color, shape, depth, texture, movement, etc. . . . in everything around you. Reflect upon all that sight has contributed to your life experience to enrich it: beauty, nonverbal communication with others, knowledge through reading and observation, protection, happiness, pleasure, etc. Try to realize how different your life . . . and you . . . would be had you been born without this sense, or had you lost it. Recognizing in all these reflections the loving gift of God, express *aloud* to Him your thanksgiving and praise.

Do the same for each of the other senses:

HEARING . . . stop for a while and really *listen,* even to the seeming silence, in reality teeming with sounds: again, reflect upon all this sense has contributed to your life experience to enrich it . . . the sound of human voices, music, etc., etc. . . . and how different your life would be without it. Recognizing in these reflections another loving gift of God, express *ALOUD* to Him your thanksgiving and praise.

TOUCH . . . the same; consciously experiencing the feeling of the sun and the air on your skin, the textures of clothing,

81

grass, trees, stones, etc. . . . the awareness of gravity through the pressure under your feet; your sense of balance through this; reflect upon the use of touch in expressing affection, in physical work, in playing musical instruments, writing activity of any kind. Imagine your life without the consciousness of this sense, etc. Express *ALOUD* your thanksgiving and praise.

TASTE . . . as above.

SMELL . . . as above. Conclude your walk by expressing thanksgiving and praise for the gift of *SENSATE LIFE,* an instrument of communication with God, His people and His world, even as it became His human instrument by Incarnation.

Recipes from Michelina
St. Lucy's Day — December 13

Quicchia/Pudding

1 lb. Wheat berries (thoroughly washed)
1 quart milk
2 oz. semi-sweet chocolate
Pinch salt
10 tbls. cornstarch and 1 cup cold water blended
   thoroughly
Sugar to taste

Cover wheat with water. Simmer until wheat splits. Add chocolate and sugar. Cook 1 hour (low, low simmer) Add milk. STIR CONSTANTLY. When mixture starts to boil SLOWLY add cornstarch mixture. Cook until thickened. Pour into a 2 quart bowl. Cool. Cover. Refrigerate.

Cauliflower with Pasta

1 flat can anchovies in oil	1 28 oz. can tomatoes
1 small onion, chopped	1 can water
2 cloves garlic, minced	1 tsp. sugar
1/3 cup raisins	salt/pepper to taste
1/4 cup pignoli nuts (optional)	1 small head cauliflower

Cut florets in pieces and cook al dente.

Sauté first 3 ingredients in 2 tsp. olive oil. Add tomatoes and other ingredients. Bring to high simmer.

Add cauliflower. Continue to simmer ¾–1 hour.

In frying pan brown ½ cup bread crumbs in 2 tsp. olive oil, stirring constantly.

Serve sauce over spaghetti. Sprinkle with bread crumbs. Enjoy!

Catherine de Hueck Doherty — December 14
Matthew 5:1–12 and Matthew 25:31–46

Catherine is another of our saints canonized not by the official Church but by the hordes of the poor and little people of Harlem, Toronto and the other places where she established her Friendship Houses.

The story of her life is fascinating — from Russian nobility to the woods of Combermere's Madonna House. Hers was a long journey lived for Jesus as her life's work gradually and surely unfolded.

Catherine embraced some very unusual vocations as the Lord led the way. She was born into nobility and exiled after the Bolsheviks took power in Russia. She was an immigrant, very unhappily married, divorced with a church annulment, single parent, happily married, vowed celibate, working mother and foundress of what has turned out to be a Religious Community producing more vocations today than many dioceses and long-established communities.

Her life is fascinating to read. Lorene Hanley Duquin has

done a remarkable job in her biography, *They Called Her the Baroness.* Catherine's passion, like Dorothy Day's, was to care for the poor and to lead people to a radical and complete living of the Gospel.

As the various stages of her life unfolded, she responded to the Spirit's call. She turned what seemed to be failure into an opportunity for growth in holiness and love. Catherine is a great model for so many of us in today's world.

We all understand the beauty and the meaning of a vocation. We know that in religious life, marriage, single life and priesthood the Lord is truly calling us to holiness. But sometimes the call of our youthful dreams and innocence changes and the Lord calls us to walk another path. Sometimes a person makes a conscious decision in deep faith and love to leave a vocation or go another way. That way becomes their *new* vocation. Divorced and single parenthood are true vocations — true ways of finding, serving and loving God when they are embraced after authentic and soul-searching discernment, and certainly when they are forced upon a person.

The person who becomes divorced must realize that being divorced becomes their new vocation and that they have to put the pieces together and walk with the Lord as best as they can. When a person makes a decision to walk another path in honesty and in truth they are doing God's will and their life is a holy vocation.

Single parenthood, widowhood, sickness, homosexuality, divorce, annulment — they are all vocations, holy lives that will give great glory to God and love to the Church. Catherine followed the call of the Spirit and did it all with great love.

The Little Mandate — the rule of her life — is a beautiful meditation this day of Advent:

Arise — go! Sell all you possess . . .
give it directly, personally to the poor.

Take up My cross (their cross) and follow Me—
going to the poor—being poor—
being one with them—one with Me.
Little—be always little... simple—poor—childlike.
Preach the Gospel *with your life—without compromise—*
Listen to the Spirit—he will lead you.
Do little things exceedingly well for love of Me.
Love—love—love, never counting the cost.
Go into the market place and stay with Me...
pray...fast...pray always...fast.
Be hidden—be a light to your neighbor's feet.
Go without fears into the depths of people's hearts....
I shall be with you.
Pray always. I will do the rest.

Las Posadas—December 16 to December 24

Las Posadas, literally "the shelters," is a beautiful novena devotion that our dear Hispanic sisters and brothers have given to the Church. While it is very popular among the Mexicans and Puerto Ricans, it is mostly found among Central and many South American countries. It has also become quite common in many North American parishes as our dear Hispanic sisters and brothers continue to enrich the Church with their beautiful faith and tradition.

Las Posadas is about the journey of Mary and Joseph on their way to Bethlehem. They stop at different shelters each night of the novena. These shelters are different homes in the community. The "holy pilgrims" (Mary and Joseph) lead the group in the home in song, special prayers and scripture readings as they prepare for the celebration of the birth of the Prince of Peace. Celebration and refreshments are always part of the gathering.

The Posadas is a popular devotion filled with meaning. As we prepare for Christmas the main concern of the Christian is whether his/her heart is ready to accept the Messiah and

Savior who comes to each of us to give us new life and hope. Each of us is the innkeeper. Will there be room in the inn this Christmas in our hearts?

We are reminded that the reason there is no room in some hearts for Jesus is because our hearts can be cluttered with so many unimportant things that prevent Jesus from finding a place. Advent is the special time to do some "house cleaning" a time to get rid of the clutter so Jesus can find a place to sit down and speak to us.

The clutter we deal with isn't necessarily sin. It can be busyness, lack of direction or priorities, or a lack of schedule. Getting rid of the clutter may be as simple as finally deciding our place and time for prayer and not varying it except for earthquake, flood, fire or war!

As we give shelter to Jesus we open our hearts to the needs and pain of our sisters and brothers. The Posadas teach us that each stranger and hurting person is the Holy Family on the way to Bethlehem. Is there room in the inn for them this Christmas?

Las Posadas ends with midnight Mass, the "Mass of the Rooster." Many churches and communities adapt the Posadas to fit their community's needs and traditions. Celebrating the traditions of so many cultures that make up the beautiful mosaic of the Church in the United States is yet another example of why we are so blessed in this country.

Meditations on the O Antiphons

(December 17 through December 23)

Luke 1 — The Magnificat

THE MAGNIFICAT is introduced each day of the year by an antiphon. An antiphon, a few words of Scripture or Scriptural reading, sets a special theme that colors the praying of the Magnificat that day. The psalms and the Benedictus of Zachary are also introduced by antiphons.

The Antiphons of the days leading up to Christmas Eve (December 17 to December 23) are among the most beautiful and most cherished of the whole year. They are truly works of art. The Latin text is concise and powerful. All translations (mine included) are limp in comparison. The O Antiphons make for touching and soul-searching prayer during these holy days as we approach the birthday of the Prince of Peace.

Every day of the year in evening prayer, the Church praises and glorifies the Lord in the Magnificat:

"Magnificat anima mea Dominum — My soul proclaims the Lord...." This Magnificat song of Mary in Luke 1 has its roots in the Hebrew scriptures but it is a prophetic voice in which Mary speaks on behalf of the "little ones" of God.

The message is clear: God is the champion of the humble and the fragile. As they place their hope in Him, He delivers them and protects them. Humility is more powerful than force and wealth. God favors those who have few worldly things but are rich in the things of the Spirit.

This song of Mary is meant to be the song of every true disciple of Jesus. It is the song we sing in gratitude to the Lord for His mercy and for all the blessings lavished upon us. This is the song we sing with Mary as we reach out to our sisters and brothers who need us. The Magnificat is the National Anthem of those who seek justice and peace for all people. This great song fills the church with a daily call to justice and repentance.

In the time of Advent we become more sensitive to the justice and peace that the Church must wage. We are educated once again that charity is vice not virtue, when it takes the place of justice. It is a hard lesson to learn, but Mary, our model, teaches it to us as we sing her Magnificat with her.

As our prayer today, let us pick up Luke 1 and slowly and lovingly pray and sing with Mary her great song, the Magnificat. We sing this song at the end of the day with countless sisters and brothers all over the world who with Mary can say: *"For He who is mighty has done great things for me and holy is His name"* (Luke 1:49).

December 17 — O Sapiéntia

O Sapiéntia, quae exóre Altíssimi prodíste,
attíngens a fíne usque ad fínem,
fórtiter suáviter disponénsque ómnia:
véni ad docéndum nos víam prudéntiae.

O Wisdom, you who have come forth from the mouth
    of the Most High,
You firmly reach from one end of the universe to the
    other,
yet gently order all things.
Come, to teach us the way of Prudence.

Jesus is here described as Wisdom. He is the Word of the Father, proceeding from Him from all eternity. The Word of the Father gently yet firmly holds all things together and calls creation to order and harmony. This order and harmony takes form in the Kingdom of God.

Jesus, the Messiah, comes to the world to bring us harmony and peace. He creates in our hearts a new kingdom, one of love, peace and dignity for each person.

The antiphon ends with a plea: "Come, and teach us the way of prudence." That's a wonderful prayer. What is prudence? Ultimately it is a way of judging and decision-making that flows from prayer, experience, consultation, meditation and of course, Wisdom, who is the Lord.

This antiphon echoes the feelings of St. Paul in Philippians 2:5: *"Have that mind in you which was in Christ Jesus."* Wisdom teaches us His mind and His way of finding reality. What we are praying for in asking to be taught the way of Wisdom is to have the mind and heart of Jesus in all that we plan, think and do. We are praying to become more and more like Jesus.

December 18 — O Adonái

O Adonái, et Dux Dómus Israel,
qui Móysi in ígne flámmae rúbi apparuísti,
et éi in Sína légem dedísti:
véni ad rediméndum nos in bráchio exténto.

O Lord Adonai and Leader of the House of Israel,
You who appeared to Moses in the burning bush,
and gave Him the Law on Mt. Sinai
come to redeem us with outstretched arms.

In this great antiphon we remember the history of our people in the process of being set free from Egypt and from the slavery of sin that shackles us now. In this time of Advent our memory goes back much further than Bethlehem, it goes back to the formation and deliverance of God's chosen people in Egypt and their march through the desert for forty years into the land flowing with milk and honey.

The great event of Mt. Sinai made Israel a covenanted people with Yahweh. He promises to be their God if they will be His people and keep the covenant. Yahweh loves His people and promises eternal fidelity and love.

The love affair between Yahweh and Israel will be a very rocky one. Over and over again Israel will break the covenant. Yahweh will again and again chastise and forgive his people and renew his promise. The drama and the passion of Yahweh for his prostitute wife (Israel) is most beautifully told in the book of Hosea.

As we read it we see our own lives, our infidelity and broken promises. We also see the changeless and passionate love of our God who will never let go of us or deny us. We see our own life story told over and over again — covenant, adultery, forgiveness, reconciliation and new beginnings.

And so this Advent we remember our past so that our future may be brighter. Come, Lord Jesus and set us free.

December 19 — O Radix Jesse

O Radix Jésse, qui stas in sígnum populórum,
super quem continébunt réges os súum,
quem géntes deprecabúntur: véni ad liberándum nos,
jam nóli tardáre.

O Root of Jesse, who stands as a sign to all people,
before whom the rulers of the earth are silent
and whom all nations adore:
come and set us free, please don't delay, come!

In this antiphon we again go back far before the Annunciation to our Jewish roots. Jesse is the father of King David. The Messiah must come from the line of David. The first chapter of the Gospel of St. Matthew presents the genealogy of Jesus — his roots and his history. Matthew presents this genealogy based on the number seven — seven is the monogram for David. The Messiah, Jesus, is the first fruit and the perfection of the yearning of all Israel. He is totally and completely a Jew. He is one in spirit and blood, faith and religion with his people. He is the long awaited one, the Messiah of Israel.

Matthew wants his readers to know that this Jesus the Messiah is truly human — one of us! Matthew had a lot of fun in this genealogy putting some very salty and unsavory people in Jesus' family tree. In this pedigree of Jesus we find Rahab, the prostitute of Jericho, Tamar the seducer and adulteress, Bathsheba the adulteress, seduced by the central figure of the Messianic line — King David, the adulterer and murderer. (He certainly had a lot of life experience for his psalms!) Jesus comes from Ruth, a Moabite, a hated and unacceptable people to Israel — not even a Jewess.

The point of this fooling around on the part of Matthew is to tell us with this literary game that Jesus comes *from* sinners *to save* sinners. His redemption is not for the righteous but for the broken and the alienated.

Matthew breaks down all the barriers. It doesn't matter whether you are Jew or Gentile, male or female, holy or wild, Jesus has come from all of us to be salvation for us and through us to the whole world.

December 20 — O Key of David

O Clávis Dávid, et scéptrum dómus Israel:
qui áperis, et némo cláudit; cláudis,
et némo áperit: véni, et éduc vínctum de dómo cárceris,
sedéntem in ténebris et úmbra mórtis.

O Key of David, and scepter of the House of Israel:
you who open and no one is able to close

you who close and no one is able to open,
come and lead out from prison those who are bound
sitting in darkness and the shadow of death.

The beautiful image of the Messiah holding the great Key is such a powerful image of Jesus coming to a world that is imprisoned by sin and hatred. The captivity that Israel suffered at different times was real and bloody. Israel yearned to be set free from captivity and humiliation and to be given the dignity of being a free and prosperous nation. The yearning for the Messiah and a great deal of national and political sentiment mingled with the religious yearnings and dreams. They yearned for a powerful Messiah before whom nations would bow down and do homage. They yearned to be on top again.

As we pray this antiphon this Advent there are many throughout the world who yearn for that liberation and freedom. There are literally millions who have suffered and are presently enduring the hell of war, ethnic cleansing, deportation, political murder (those who have disappeared). The list of death and torture and war-related agonies fills the papers each day.

So many others suffer their personal slaveries in addictions of all kinds. They yearn for liberation and peace. They pray to be set free from lives that are never happy.

Come, Lord Jesus. Come to your people and set us free. Lead us all from the personal prisons that hold us as we sit in darkness and the shadow of death awaiting new life. This Christmas may the lamb and the lion lie down together in peace.

December 21 —O Oriens

O Oriens, spléndor lúcis aetérnae,
et sol justítiae: véni, et illúmina sedéntes
in ténebris et úmbra mórtis.

O Rising Sun, splendor of eternal light,
and sun of justice, come, and give light
to those sitting in darkness and the shadow of death.

One of the most emotional and moving moments in the life of a parish is to be gathered on the beach on Easter morning at 6:00 a.m. —after having celebrated a four-hour Easter Vigil — celebrating the Easter Sunrise Mass and seeing the glorious and powerful sun actually rise. Talk about the glory and the majesty of God!

The O Antiphon describes the Lord Jesus in terms of that glorious and eternal light. He is a Lord who casts out all darkness forever. There are no more shadows or darkness when Jesus is present shining in our lives. This Jesus casts away the shadows of fear, suspicion, hate and envy. He is the light shining in the darkness —a darkness that has never been able to put this Light out (John 1). It is the light of God's Love.

Advent is an invitation to God's people to leave behind death, darkness and shadows. There is never a reason to remain in the shadows as Jesus invites us to live in the light and the glory of His love. This call to the light is a call to love ourselves in a new way. Nothing gives us greater joy and happiness than to live the way Jesus has called us to live.

We are not punished *for* our hatred, greed, gluttony, lust, envy, sloth, pride; rather, they punish us. They cause us unhappiness and they take away our peace.

Jesus calls us to the light because we need and deserve His peace and happiness. To live as if each day is our last day; to be at peace with the Lord and every one in this world — that is what He wants for His holy people.

Come, Lord Jesus. Bring us out of the darkness and break our chains.

December 22 — O Rex Géntium

O Rex géntium, et desiderátus eárum,
lapísque anguláris, qui fácis útraque únum:
véni, et sálva hóminem, quem de límo formásti.

O King of Nations, the one for whom all people long,
the great cornerstone, who makes of us all one;
come, and save the human family
which you formed from the clay.

This magnificent antiphon speaks of Jesus as the long desired one. The one for whom our ancestors yearned. The
one who would set them free from slavery, bondage and
tyranny. The long desired one who would finally bring about
peace and the establishment of a Kingdom of Justice. The
long awaited one would truly change the instruments of war
into instruments of farming and peace.

As much as we identify these sentiments with our ancestors, they are felt by more people today in economic and
political slavery than by all the people who lived in the
time of Israel awaiting the Messiah. The incredible truth is
that the emotions and experiences of Israel expressed in
the scriptures are truer today and more applicable today
than ever!

The human family yearns for peace and justice, an end
to war and bombing and land mines and resettlements and
ethnic cleansing. The world yearns for peace, that peace
that only the Lord can bring.

We have to reflect in this holy time on how we personally — by our prayers, our work and our vote — can bring
peace and justice to our world. Advent means change of
heart and conversion. I must personally embrace peacemak-
ing in my heart and in my life. That is the beginning of the
Messianic Kingdom for my neighbor.

Jesus, the great cornerstone, holds us all together. The cornerstone of the Church is not an ornament. It is the very

heart of all that we are and all that we do. Jesus is the center. Jesus is the heart. In these holy days we are called to put Him back in the center of our lives.

December 23 — O Emmánuel

O Emmánuel, Rex et légifer nóster,
exspectátio géntium, et Salvátor eárum:
véni ad salvándum nos Dómine Déus nóster.

O Emmanuel, Our King and Lawgiver,
the long awaited one of all the nations and their Saviour:
Come, O Lord Our God and save us.

Today in the final O Antiphon before Christmas Eve and Day we address the Messiah King, the Lord Jesus with his magnificent title: Emmanuel — God with us.

We do well today to ponder and pray over that most glorious of all titles — God with us. The Incarnation changed all of human history. When Mary said her "yes" to the archangel Gabriel all of life and history changed. At her "yes" God dwelt among us in the womb of the Virgin. Our way of looking at, thinking about and speaking of God changed radically, never to return to what it was before.

Our God was no longer the one so far away and transcendent. Our God was truly Emmanuel God with us. He was flesh of our flesh and bone of our bone. He was no longer just the God of Sinai and the Torah, now he was the baby growing within Mary's womb, truly the Word of the Father and truly the fruit of Mary's womb.

This Jesus who would be born to us on Christmas would come to us in humility and poverty. The little baby so helpless in Mary's arms would astound believers for generations to come. They would look at Him and say: This is God — He's not so bad after all! I'm not afraid of Him.

And that is God's hope for the human family; that all would look upon the baby and see nothing but love, tenderness and gentleness; that our God will know that we could never be afraid again and never keep Him at a distance. There is only one response we have when we come into the presence of a baby — to take that baby in our arms, hold him, caress him, kiss him, sing to him — love him. That's what our God hopes that you will do to Him this Christmas and always. Our Jesus is Emmanuel — God with us — a little baby.